DAY HIKES IN
SAN LUIS OBISPO COUNTY
CALIFORNIA

by Robert Stone

Day Hike Books, Inc.
RED LODGE, MONTANA

Published by Day Hike Books, Inc.
P.O. Box 865
Red Lodge, Montana 59068

Distributed by The Globe Pequot Press
246 Goose Lane
P.O. Box 480
Guilford, CT 06437-0480
800-243-0495 (direct order) · 800-820-2329 (fax order)
www.globe-pequot.com

Photographs by Robert Stone
Design by Paula Doherty

The author has made every attempt to provide
accurate information in this book. The author and publisher do
not assume any responsibility for loss, damage or injury caused
through the use of this book. Please let this book guide you,
but be aware that each hiker assumes responsibility
for their own safety.

Cover photo: San Simeon Bay Trail—Hike 3
Back cover photo: Bob Jones City to the Sea Bike Trail—Hike 56

TABLE OF CONTENTS

About the Hikes. 6
Map of the Hikes. 8

— THE HIKES —

San Simeon, Cambria and Cayucos

1. Salmon Creek Trail to Salmon Creek Falls 10
2. Ragged Point—Cliffside Trail and Nature Trail 12
3. San Simeon Bay Trail 14
4. San Simeon State Park—San Simeon Trail 16
5. Moonstone Beach Trail. 18
6. East West Ranch Bluff Trail. 20
7. Whale Rock Reservoir. 22

Paso Robles to Atascadero

8. Lake Nacimiento—Shoreline Trail 24
9. Lake Nacimiento—Oak Knoll and Quail's Roost Trail. 26
10. Salinas River from Lawrence Moore Park 28
11. Anza National Historic Trail—North 30
12. Anza National Historic Trail—South 32
13. Heilman Regional Park—Jim Green Trail 34
14. Cerro Alto Loop Trail. 36
15. Cerro Alto Summit 38

Morro Bay, Baywood Park and Los Osos

Map of Hikes 16—33. 40
16. Cloisters Wetland to Morro Rock 42
17. Morro Bay State Park—Black Hill 44
18. Morro Bay State Park—Chorro Hill. 46
19. Morro Bay State Park—Portola Point. 48
20. Morro Bay State Park—Quarry and Park Ridge Loop 50

21. Morro Bay State Park—Crespi Trail 52
22. Elfin Forest Natural Area 54
23. Sweet Springs Nature Preserve 56
24. Los Osos Oaks State Reserve. 58

Montaña de Oro State Park

25. Morro Bay Sand Spit. 60
26. Dunes Trail to Hazard Canyon Reef 62
27. Ridge Trail to Hazard Peak. 64
28. Islay Creek Trail 66
29. Reservoir Flats Trail 68
30. Oats Peak Trail 70
31. Valencia Peak Trail. 72
32. Bluff Trail 74
33. Coon Creek Trail 76

San Luis Obispo

Map of Hikes 34—48 78
34. El Chorro County Regional Park
    Dairy Creek and El Chorro Loop. 80
35. El Chorro County Regional Park
    Eagle Rock and Oak Woodlands Loop 82
36. Felsman Loop Trail. 84
37. Bishop Peak. 86
38. Cerro San Luis Obispo 88
39. Laguna Lake Trail 90
40. South Hills Trail. 92
41. Terrace Hill 94
42. Yucca Ridge Trail 96
43. Poly Canyon Design Village 98
44. Poly Canyon 100
45. Reservoir Canyon Trail 102
46. Stagecoach Road to Cuesta Pass 104
47. West Cuesta Ridge Road to Botanical Area 106
48. East Cuesta Ridge Road 108

Santa Margarita

49. Santa Margarita Lake—Grey Pine Trail to Eagle View ... 110
50. Santa Margarita Lake—Lone Pine Trail to Vaca Flat...... 111
51. Rinconada Trail 114
52. Santa Margarita Lake—Sandstone Trail 116
53. Santa Margarita Lake—Blinn Ranch Trail............... 118

Avila Beach, Shell Beach, Pismo Beach Grover Beach and Oceano

54. Pecho Coast Trail.................................... 120
55. Cave Landing and Pirate's Cove 122
56. Bob Jones City to the Sea Bike Trail 124
57. Shell Beach Bluffs Walking Path 126
58. Chumash Park 128
59. Monarch Butterfly Grove and Meadow Creek Trail.... 130
60. Oceano Lagoon—Guiton Trail....................... 132
61. Pismo Dunes 134

Arroyo Grande and Nipomo

62. Lopez Lake—
    Blackberry Springs and Turkey Ridge Loop 136
63. Lopez Lake—Cougar Trail 138
64. Lopez Lake—High Ridge Trail 140
65. Lopez Lake—Marina and Rocky Point Trails.......... 142
66. Lopez Lake—
    Tuouski and Two Waters Trails to Duna Vista 144
67. Little Falls Trail 146
68. Big Falls Trail 148
69. Hi Mountain Trail 150
70. Trout Creek Trail 152
71. Oso Flaco Lake Trail 154
72. Nipomo Regional Park.............................. 156

About the Hikes

San Luis Obispo County, California, sits between the white sand beaches of Santa Barbara County to the south and the dramatic coastal cliffs of Monterey County to the north. The county's 84 miles of spectacular coastline includes wide, sandy beaches; drifting, windswept, coastal dunes; rocky coves; jagged bluffs; grassy coastal terraces; protected bays and tidepools; wildlife sanctuaries; and a fertile, 1,400-acre estuary.

Heading inland from the Pacific Ocean are oak-studded hills, verdant farmland, pristine mountain lakes and the Santa Lucia Range of the Los Padres National Forest. A chain of nine extinct volcanoes, which are 23 million years old, form a spine of peaks extending from the city of San Luis Obispo to the ocean at Morro Bay. San Luis Obispo rests in a beautiful valley amongst these volcanic morros and the rolling foothills of the Santa Lucia Mountain Range.

The beautiful landscape in San Luis Obispo County is a hiker's paradise. Within the unique and diverse terrain of the county's many parks, mountains, wilderness areas and coastline is an extensive network of hiking trails to accommodate every level of hiking expertise. The hikes in this guide stretch along the Pacific Coast to the Los Padres National Forest, taking you to waterfalls, ocean bluffs, coastal sand dunes, lakes, rivers, swimming holes, canyons, extraordinary rock formations, caves, mountain peaks, rolling meadows and panoramic views.

Montaña de Oro State Park, one of the county's major parks, encompasses 8,400 acres with 7 miles of coastline. The mostly undeveloped park has towering coastal peaks, jagged cliffs, grassy bluffs, reefs, coves, caves, sand dunes, eucalyptus groves and stream-fed canyons. There are more than 50 miles of hiking trails. Included in this guide are nine great hikes from the park.

The hikes in this guide are divided into eight distinct regions, taking you to 72 of the best day hikes throughout the county.

Each hike is designed to get you to the trailhead and onto the trail with clear, concise directions. To help you decide which hikes are most appealing to you, a brief summary of the highlights is included with each hike. You may want to enjoy these areas for the whole day.

Most of the hikes are found within a short drive of the cities. An overall map of the county and the hikes can be found on pages 8—9. An enlarged map of hikes from Morro Bay to Montaña de Oro State Park is on pages 40—41 and a map around the city of San Luis Obispo is on pages 78—79.

Each of these hikes is also accompanied with its own map and detailed driving and hiking directions. U.S.G.S. maps and other supplementary maps are also listed with the hikes but are not necessary. Many of the U.S.G.S. maps have not been updated recently, and the trails may not be shown. However, these maps are interesting and useful because they show the topography of the region.

From one end of San Luis Obispo County to the other, there is a range of great sights and hikes. Whichever area you choose to visit, this county is rich in beauty and diversity, waiting for you to discover it out on the trails.

A note of caution: Ticks are prolific throughout the county and poison oak flourishes in canyons and shady moist areas. Be prepared with insect repellent, hydro-cortisone cream, drinking water and sunscreen, and be sure to wear comfortable hiking shoes.

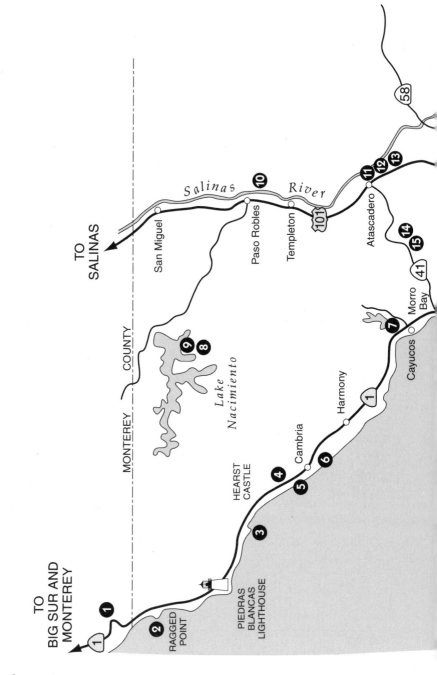

TO
BIG SUR AND
MONTEREY

TO
SALINAS

Salinas *River*

San Miguel

Paso Robles

Templeton

101

Atascadero

58

Morro
Bay

Cayucos

Harmony

Cambria

HEARST
CASTLE

Lake
Nacimiento

MONTEREY ---- COUNTY

RAGGED
POINT

PIEDRAS
BLANCAS
LIGHTHOUSE

41

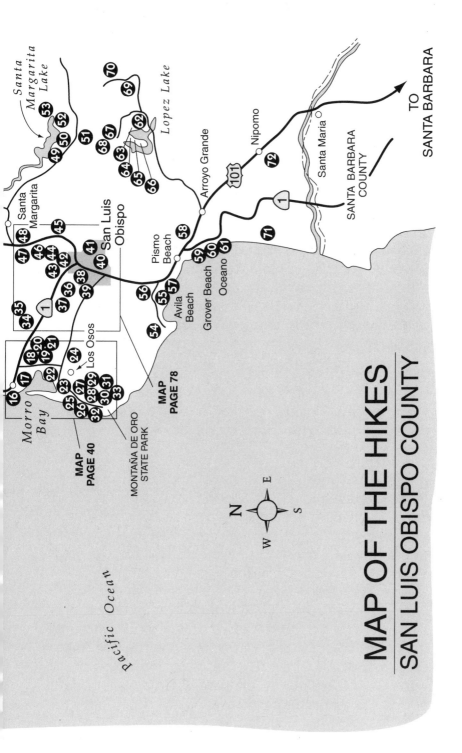

MAP OF THE HIKES
SAN LUIS OBISPO COUNTY

Hike 1
Salmon Creek Trail to Salmon Creek Falls

Hiking distance: 0.6 miles round trip
Hiking time: 20 minutes
Elevation gain: 150 feet
Maps: U.S.G.S. Burro Mountain

Summary of hike: Salmon Creek Trail is at the southern end of Big Sur country in Monterey County, 2.2 miles north of the county line. A waterfall this dynamic and so close to San Luis Obispo County had to be included. A short hike leads to Salmon Creek Falls, where a tremendous amount of rushing water plunges from three chutes. The water drops more than 100 feet off the Santa Lucia Mountains onto the rocks and pools. Under the shady landscape of alders and laurels, a cool mist sprays over the mossy green streamside vegetation.

Driving directions: From Cambria, drive 26 miles north on Highway 1 to the signed Salmon Creek trailhead on the right. The turn-off is 3.7 miles north of the Ragged Point Inn at a horseshoe bend in the road. Park on the right in the parking pullout.

Hiking directions: Walk alongside the guardrail to the signed trailhead on the south side of Salmon Creek. Salmon Creek Falls can be seen from the guardrail. Take the Salmon Creek Trail up the gorge into the lush, verdant forest. Pass an old wooden gate and cross a small tributary stream. Two hundred yards ahead is a signed junction. The right fork continues on the Salmon Creek Trail, leading up to Spruce Camp and Estrella Camp, primitive streamside campsites two and three miles ahead. Take the left fork towards the falls. Cross another small stream, then descend around huge boulders towards Salmon Creek at the base of the falls. The thunderous sound of the waterfall will lead you to the base. Climb around the wet boulders to various caves and overlooks.

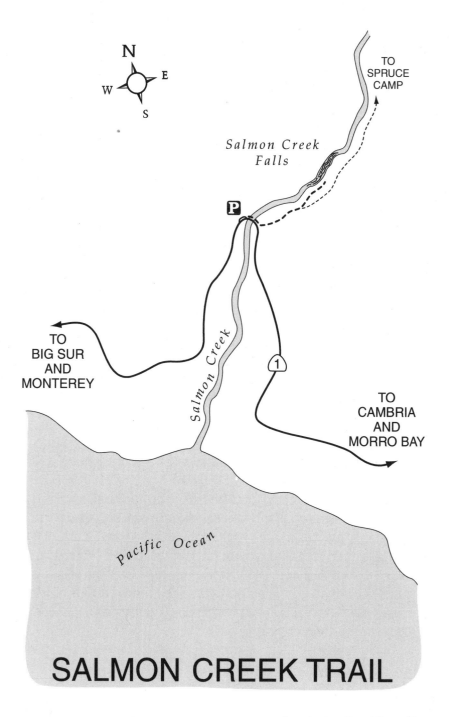

SALMON CREEK TRAIL

Hike 2
Ragged Point
Cliffside Trail and Nature Trail

Hiking distance: 1 mile round trip
Hiking time: 30 minutes
Elevation gain: 300 feet
Maps: U.S.G.S. Burro Mountain

Summary of hike: The Ragged Point Cliffside Trail cuts across the edge of the steep, rugged, north-facing cliff where the San Luis Obispo coast turns into the Big Sur coast. The Cliffside Trail ends at the black sand beach and rocky shore at the base of Black Swift Falls, a 300-foot tiered waterfall. Benches are perched on the cliff for great views of the sheer coastal mountains plunging into the sea. The Ragged Point Nature Trail follows the perimeter of the peninsula along the high blufftop terrace. There are scenic vista points and an overlook platform.

Driving directions: From Cambria, drive 23 miles north on Highway 1 to the Ragged Point Inn and Restaurant on the left. Turn left and park in the paved lot.

Hiking directions: Take the graveled path west (between the snack bar and gift shop) towards the point. Fifty yards ahead is a signed junction at a grassy overlook. The Nature Trail continues straight ahead, circling the blufftop terrace through windswept pine and cypress trees. At the northwest point is a viewing platform. Waterfalls can be seen cascading off the cliffs on both sides of the promontory. Back at the junction, the Cliffside Trail descends down the steps over the cliff's edge past a bench and across a wooden bridge. Switchbacks cut across the edge of the steep cliff to the base of Black Swift Falls at the sandy beach. After enjoying the surroundings head back up the steep path.

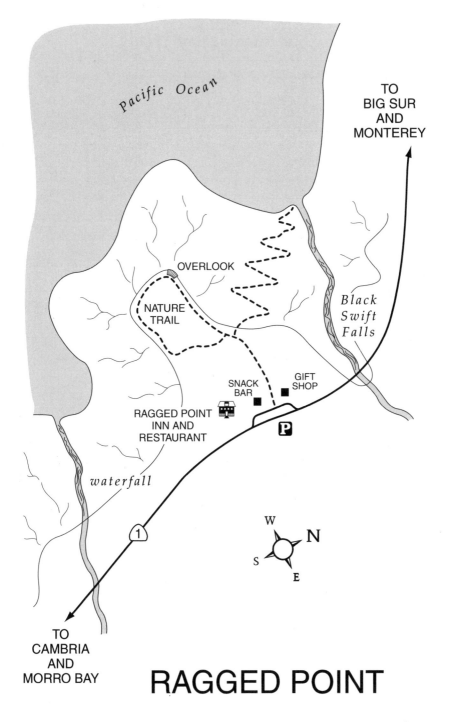

Pacific Ocean

TO
BIG SUR
AND
MONTEREY

OVERLOOK

NATURE
TRAIL

*Black
Swift
Falls*

SNACK
BAR

GIFT
SHOP

RAGGED POINT
INN AND
RESTAURANT

P

waterfall

①

W **N**

S

E

TO
CAMBRIA
AND
MORRO BAY

RAGGED POINT

Hike 3
San Simeon Bay Trail

Hiking distance: 2.5 miles round trip
Hiking time: 1 hour
Elevation gain: 50 feet
Maps: U.S.G.S. San Simeon

Summary of hike: The San Simeon Bay Trail begins at William R. Hearst State Beach along a crescent of white sand. The hike leads to the tip of San Simeon Point, a peninsula extending a half mile into the ocean. At the point are beach coves, dramatic rock formations and tidepools (cover photo). The trail follows the bluffs through a beautiful forest of eucalyptus, pine, cedar and cypress trees.

Driving directions: From Cambria, drive 8 miles north on Highway 1 to William R. Hearst State Beach on the left, across from the turnoff to Hearst Castle. Turn left on San Simeon Road and park 0.2 miles ahead (before crossing the bridge). Pullouts are on both sides of the road by the eucalyptus grove.

Hiking directions: Walk through the entrance in the chainlink fence, and follow the path through the eucalyptus grove to the ocean, just west of the pier. Head west along the sand and cross Arroyo del Puerto Creek. Continue towards the forested point. As the beach curves south, take the distinct footpath up to the wooded bluffs. Follow the path through the eucalyptus grove along the edge of the bluffs overlooking the ocean. At the beginning of San Simeon Point, the path joins an unpaved road. Head south across the peninsula to the southeast tip. Various trails lead around the point to endless vistas, beach coves, rock formations and tidepools. The trail continues around the west side of the peninsula through tall cedar and cypress trees, forming a dark shaded tunnel. This is the turnaround spot. Return along the same path.

To hike further, the trail reemerges on the bluffs and descends onto dunes to the beach.

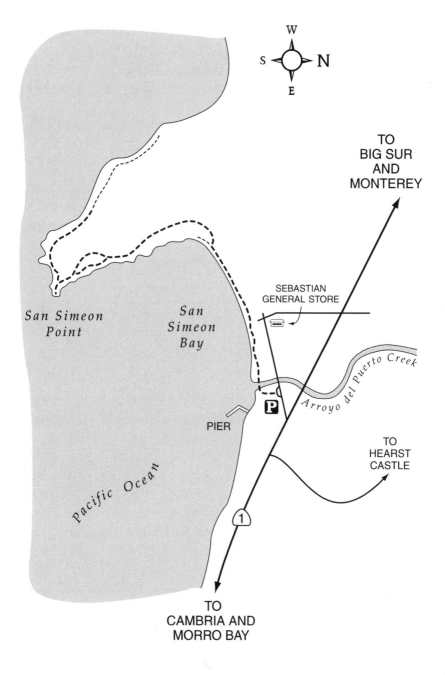

SAN SIMEON BAY TRAIL

Hike 4
San Simeon Trail
San Simeon State Park

Hiking distance: 4 mile loop
Hiking time: 2 hours
Elevation gain: 200 feet
Maps: U.S.G.S. Cambria

Summary of hike: The San Simeon Trail leads through a diverse landscape of coastal scrub, grassy meadows, wetlands, a Monterey pine forest, a eucalyptus grove and riparian woodlands. This loop hike includes footbridges and boardwalks, interpretive displays, outcroppings, vernal pools of winter rainfall, benches and Whitaker Flats, an 1800s ranch site.

Driving directions: From Highway 1 in Cambria, drive 2 miles north to the San Simeon State Park turnoff on the right. Turn right and park in the Washburn Day Use Area parking lot.

Hiking directions: Follow the wooden boardwalk east to the campground access road and bridge. Bear right on the signed gravel path through the coastal scrub. Cross a footbridge over the wetlands to the edge of the forested hillside. Ascend steps and follow the ridge east through the forest of Monterey pines. At one mile, the path descends down the hillside into Fern Gully, a lush riparian area. Cross the valley floor on Willow Bridge, a long footbridge over the stream and marshland under a canopy of trees. Continue across the grassy slope along the eastern park boundary to a trail fork at the Washburn Campground. The left fork parallels the campground road, returning to the trailhead. Take the right fork across a grassy mesa to a bench and overlook at the Mima Mounds and vernal pools. Bear left, traversing the hillside above San Simeon Creek to a massive forested outcropping. Continue past the formation and head downhill into a eucalyptus grove. Ascend the hillside, joining the trail from the campground. Bear right, parallel to the campground road, back to the trailhead.

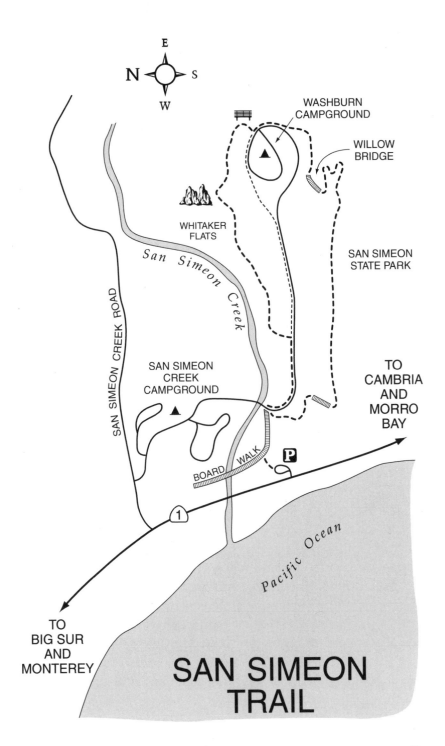

N E S W

WASHBURN
CAMPGROUND

WILLOW
BRIDGE

WHITAKER
FLATS

San Simeon Creek

SAN SIMEON CREEK ROAD

SAN SIMEON
STATE PARK

SAN SIMEON
CREEK
CAMPGROUND

TO
CAMBRIA
AND
MORRO
BAY

BOARD WALK

P

1

Pacific Ocean

TO
BIG SUR
AND
MONTEREY

SAN SIMEON
TRAIL

Hike 5
Moonstone Beach Trail

Hiking distance: 2.5 miles round trip
Hiking time: 1.5 hours
Elevation gain: Level
Maps: U.S.G.S. Cambria

Summary of hike: The Moonstone Beach Trail follows the rocky shoreline at the edge of the windswept ocean cliffs in Cambria. On the 20-foot eroded bluffs along the oceanfront corridor, several staircases lead down to the sandy beach. Along the shore are smooth, translucent, milky white moonstone agates. The trail leads past small coves, rock formations and tidepools to scenic overlooks. There are views up the coast to San Simeon Point and the Piedras Blancas Lighthouse. This is an excellent vantage point to watch migrating gray whales.

Driving directions: From Highway 1 in Cambria, turn west on Windsor Boulevard and a quick right onto Moonstone Beach Drive. Continue 0.3 miles to the Santa Rosa Creek parking lot on the left. Turn left and park.

Hiking directions: The trail begins near the mouth of Santa Rosa Creek on the north end of the parking lot. Head north on the sandstone bluffs overlooking the ocean, parallel to Moonstone Beach Drive. Steps descend to the sandy beach. Return up to the bluffs, crossing small wooden footbridges. At one mile, the old highway bridge spans Leffingwell Creek. Bear left down a ramp to the beach and cross the sand. Ascend the grassy slope to a picnic area and cypress grove at Leffingwell Landing, part of San Simeon State Beach. Cross the parking lot, picking up the trail again on the bluffs, and wind through groves of Monterey pine and cypress. At 1.5 miles is an overlook on the left at the north end of Moonstone Beach Drive. Past the overlook, steps lead down to the beach. Return along the same path.

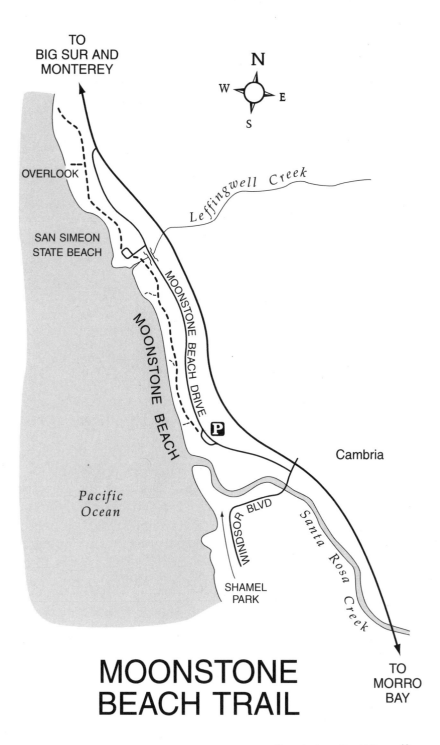

MOONSTONE
BEACH TRAIL

Hike 6
East West Ranch Bluff Trail

Hiking distance: 2 miles round trip
Hiking time: 1 hour
Elevation gain: Level
Maps: U.S.G.S. Cambria

Summary of hike: The East West Ranch Bluff Trail in Cambria follows the edge of the eroded bluffs above the ocean. The rocky shore and tidepools can be seen below. There are two bridge crossings, a handcrafted wooden shelter and several unique benches. The one-mile long trail crosses a private ranch from Windsor Boulevard in the south to Windsor Boulevard in the north. There is no beach access on the trail, but the views are fantastic.

Driving directions: From Highway 1 in Cambria, head south on Burton Drive. Go 0.3 miles to Ardath Drive and turn right. Drive 0.7 miles to Madison Street and bear right. Continue 0.2 miles to Orlando Drive and turn left. Go 0.2 miles to Windsor Boulevard and turn right. Park one block ahead at the end of the road.

Hiking directions: Head north through the trailhead gate and cross the flat grassy bluffs that overlook the jagged shoreline, tidepools and the ocean. Cross the wooden foot-bridge over a stream. The trail curves along the edge of the eroded bluffs. Cross a second bridge, then head past benches and a wooden shelter. The trail ends by a fenceline at the southern edge of a residential neighborhood. Return along the same trail.

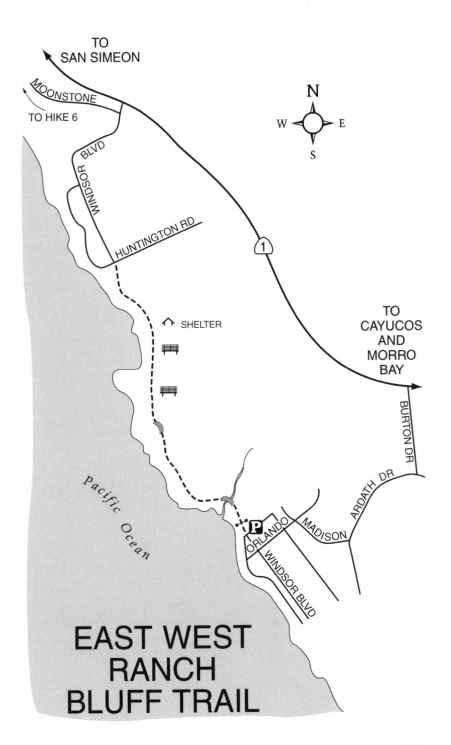

TO
SAN SIMEON

MOONSTONE
TO HIKE 6

WINDSOR BLVD

HUNTINGTON RD

1

N
W E
S

⌂ SHELTER

TO
CAYUCOS
AND
MORRO
BAY

BURTON DR

ARDATH DR

Pacific Ocean

P

ORLANDO

MADISON

WINDSOR BLVD

EAST WEST RANCH BLUFF TRAIL

Hike 7
Whale Rock Reservoir

Open from the last Saturday in April — November 15
Wednesday through Sunday and holidays

Hiking distance: 3.8 miles round trip
Hiking time: 2 hours
Elevation gain: 50 feet
Maps: U.S.G.S. Morro Bay North and Cayucos

Summary of hike: Whale Rock Reservoir is open to the public during the trout fishing season. The trail alongside the lake is primarily used as a fishing access, but is also a beautiful area for hiking and picnicking. The Whale Rock Dam was built in 1961, creating the 1,350-acre reservoir. It is a domestic water supply used as a source of drinking water. The lake is fed from Old Creek and Cottontail Creek at the two northern points. The lake is surrounded by grassy rolling hills.

Driving directions: From Highway 1 at the south end of Cayucos, take Old Creek Road 1.5 miles northeast to the Whale Rock Reservoir parking area on the left, just before the PG&E substation. An entrance fee is required.

Hiking directions: Walk through the entrance gate to the trailhead sign. The left fork leads 0.2 miles on the wide grassy path to the fenced border at Johnson Cove. The right fork leads past a picnic area, then follows the curves of the lake parallel to the shoreline. The path frequently rises above the lake and drops back to the waterline. At 1.3 miles, the trail curves around Dead Horse Cove to a trail split. The right fork is a secondary fishing access from a parking lot by Old Creek Road. Bear left and loop around the perimeter of Dead Horse Point. The trail ends at a fenceline north of the point. Return on the same trail.

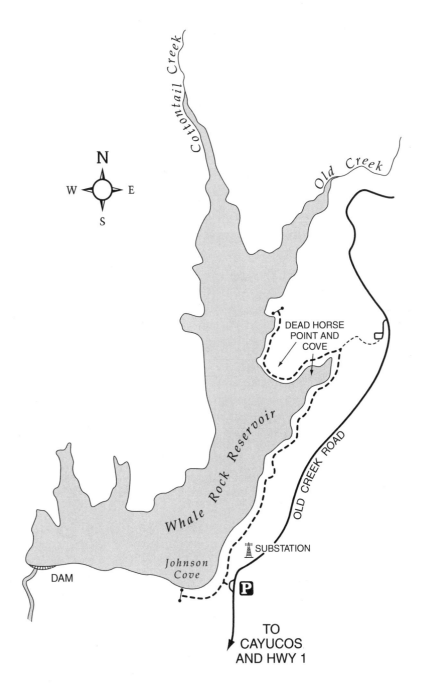

WHALE ROCK RESERVOIR

Hike 8
Shoreline Trail
Lake Nacimiento

Hiking distance: 4.6 miles round trip
Hiking time: 2.5 hours
Elevation gain: 400 feet
Maps: U.S.G.S. Tierra Redonda Mountain and Lime Mountain
      Lake Nacimiento Resort trail map

Summary of hike: The Shoreline Trail follows the contours of the serene rolling hills above the east side of Lake Nacimiento. The pastoral grassy countryside is spotted with ponderosa pines and oak trees. The trail rarely gets close to the shoreline but always overlooks the beautiful lake.

Driving directions: From Highway 101 in Paso Robles, take the 24th Street/Highway 46 East exit. Head west on 24th Street through Paso Robles, and drive 16 miles to the Lake Nacimiento Dam at a road fork. (24th Street becomes Nacimiento Lake Drive.) Bear left and drive 0.7 miles to the entrance station. Continue a quarter mile to the trailhead parking pullout on the left at a vista point. An entrance fee is required.

Hiking directions: Walk past the trail sign, heading up a short rise while overlooking the lake. Cross the rolling meadow dotted with trees. Loop around the edge of a forested ravine to an unpaved ranch road. Bear right and pick up the footpath on the right 30 yards ahead. Descend through an oak grove, and follow the hillside trail 150 feet above the lake. At one mile is a signed junction. The right fork descends to the shoreline to a fishing access. The main trail curves left to a saddle and rejoins the old road. Bear right along the road to a footpath at the base of a hill. The path zigzags down to a beach in a secluded cove. The main trail follows the road a short distance to a road fork. Curve right and follow the ridge to a vista point on a peninsula. Head downhill to the flat beach area at the point. Return along the same trail.

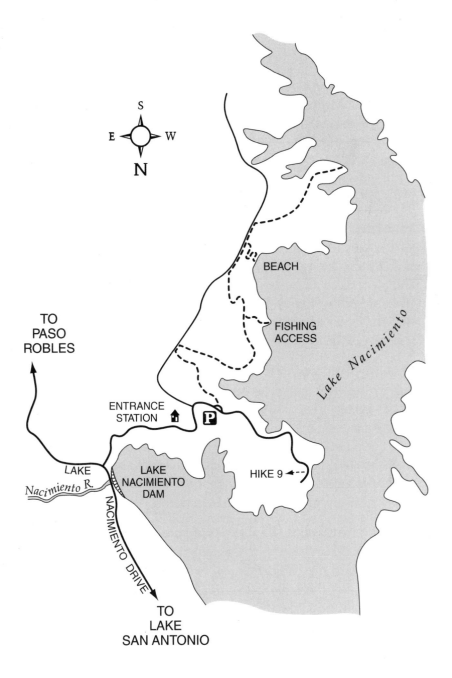

S

E W

N

TO
PASO
ROBLES

BEACH

FISHING
ACCESS

Lake Nacimiento

ENTRANCE
STATION

P

LAKE
Nacimiento R.

HIKE 9

LAKE
NACIMIENTO
DAM

NACIMIENTO DRIVE

TO
LAKE
SAN ANTONIO

SHORELINE TRAIL

Hike 9
Oak Knoll and Quail's Roost Trail
Lake Nacimiento

Hiking distance: 1.5 miles round trip
Hiking time: 45 minutes
Elevation gain: 100 feet
Maps: U.S.G.S. Tierra Redonda Mountain
         Lake Nacimiento Resort trail map

Summary of hike: Lake Nacimiento is the county's largest reservoir. The 16-mile-long lake, nestled in a tree studded valley, was formed by a dam on the Nacimiento River. It is a popular recreation area with 165 miles of shoreline. The Oak Knoll and Quail's Roost Trail is a connector trail to the various lakeside campgrounds. The trail winds through beautiful stands of oaks and pines with great views of Lake Nacimiento and the Nacimiento Dam.

Driving directions: From Highway 101 in Paso Robles, take the 24th Street/Highway 46 East exit. Head west on 24th Street through Paso Robles, and drive 16 miles to the Lake Nacimiento Dam at a road fork. (24th Street becomes Nacimiento Lake Drive outside of Paso Robles.) Bear left and drive 0.7 miles to the entrance station. Continue 0.8 miles to the boat launch parking lot. Park at the east end of the lot, farthest from the water's edge. An entrance fee is required.

Hiking directions: Walk across the park road, and enter the restricted parking lot to the signed trailhead. The wide path winds around the hillside through groves of ponderosa pine and oak trees. Curve around several drainages and lake overlooks to the park road. Take the road 50 yards to the right, picking up the signed trail on the left. Follow the forested path east on the narrow fire road. The trail ends at the road by the Oak Knoll and Quail's Roost Campgrounds. Return by following the same path back. *

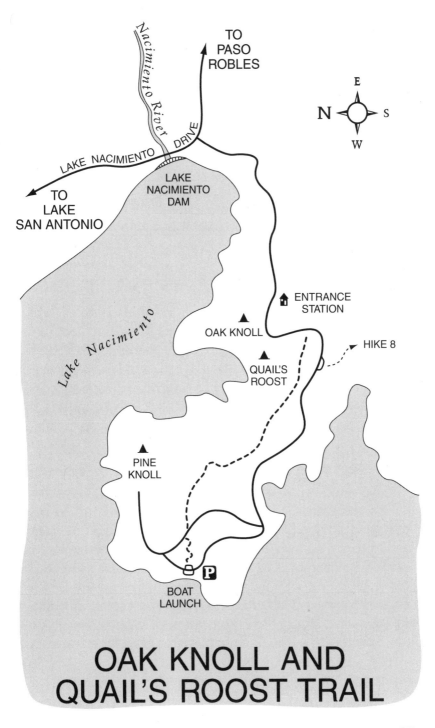

OAK KNOLL AND QUAIL'S ROOST TRAIL

Hike 10
Salinas River
from Lawrence Moore Park

Hiking distance: 1 mile round trip
Hiking time: 40 minutes
Elevation gain: Level
Maps: U.S.G.S. Templeton
The Thomas Guide—San Luis Obispo County

Summary of hike: The Salinas River area in Paso Robles has an undesignated walking trail through the riparian habitat. The path leads through cottonwood, willow and sycamore groves along the banks of the river. This is a popular bird-watching trail. Migrating species frequent the area in winter and spring.

Driving directions: From Highway 101 in Paso Robles, take the Spring Street exit and drive 0.5 miles to Niblick Road. Turn right and go 0.6 miles, crossing over the Salinas River to South River Road. Turn right and continue 0.3 miles to Riverbank Lane. Turn right and drive 0.4 miles through a residential neighborhood to Lawrence Moore Park on the right. Park alongside the curb across from Bridgegate Lane.

Hiking directions: Take the unsigned but well-defined trail across the grassy flat towards the Salinas River. Descend through scrub brush, oaks and sycamores to the streambed. Follow the Salinas River downstream 0.4 miles north to the trail's end at the Niblick Road bridge on the banks of the river. Just before trail's end, a side path bears right to a wide sandy path, extending the hike a short distance through a forested grove. On the return, watch for a distinct trail on the left, which crosses the grassy flat to a paved walking path at the north end of Lawrence Moore Park. The left fork ends at a circular turnaround by the mall. The right fork returns to the trailhead.

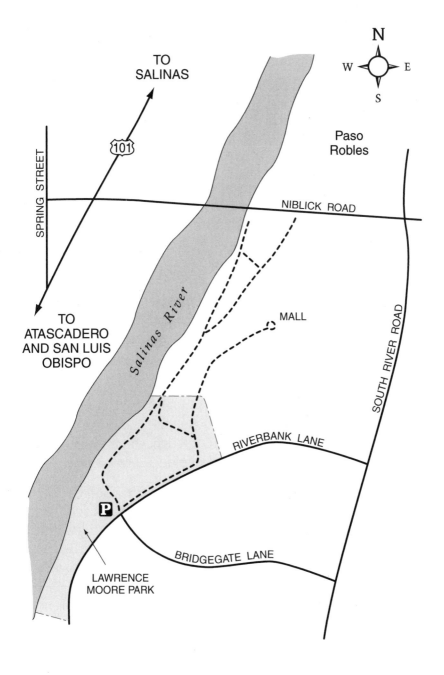

TO
SALINAS

101

SPRING STREET

TO
ATASCADERO
AND SAN LUIS
OBISPO

Salinas River

N
W   E
S

Paso
Robles

NIBLICK ROAD

MALL

SOUTH RIVER ROAD

RIVERBANK LANE

P

BRIDGEGATE LANE

LAWRENCE
MOORE PARK

SALINAS RIVER

Hike 11
Anza National Historic Trail—North

Hiking distance: 5.8 miles round trip
Hiking time: 3 hours
Elevation gain: Level
Maps: U.S.G.S. Atascadero and Templeton
      Juan Bautista de Anza National Historic Trail map

Summary of hike: The Anza National Historic Trail follows a portion of the original route led by Juan Bautista de Anza in 1776. The expedition brought hundreds of settlers and more than a thousand head of livestock from Sonora, Mexico to Alta, California. This hike follows the path along the designated northern segment of the multi-purpose hiking, biking, birding and equestrian trail. The trail winds through stands of cottonwoods, oaks, sycamores and willows, parallel to the southern banks of the Salinas River. Spanish moss hangs over the limbs of the trees.

Driving directions: From Highway 101 in Atascadero, take the Curbaril Avenue exit and head 1.3 miles east, crossing the railroad tracks to Sycamore Road. Bear left and drive 1.7 miles to the signed trailhead access on the right (on the north side of 4545 Sycamore Road). Park alongside the road.

Hiking directions: Take the water company access road east (between the houses) to the trailhead gate. Bear left on the unpaved road and head northwest. At one mile is a road split at a well house. Take the left fork a hundred yards to a fenced home and trail fork. Bear right, continuing northwest. Various side paths branch off the main route. At 2.7 miles, pass through a shady oak grove to a trail loop near the railroad tracks. Return along the same path.

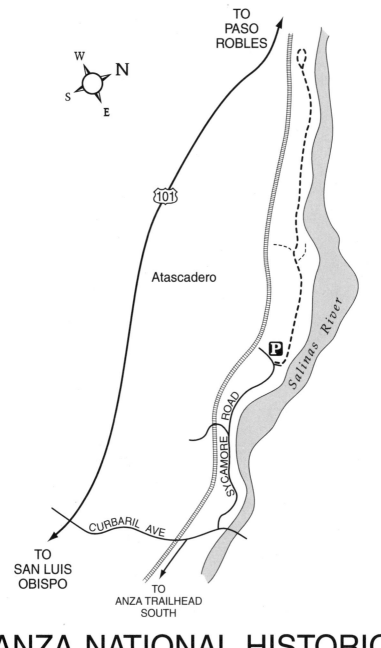

ANZA NATIONAL HISTORIC TRAIL—NORTH

Hike 12
Anza National Historic Trail—South

Hiking distance: 2.2 miles round trip
Hiking time: 1.5 hours
Elevation gain: Level
Maps: U.S.G.S. Atascadero
        Juan Bautista de Anza National Historic Trail map

Summary of hike: The Anza National Historic Trail follows a portion of the original route from Sonora, Mexico to Alta, California led by Juan Bautista de Anza more than two hundred years ago. The expedition brought hundreds of settlers and more than a thousand head of livestock. This hike follows the designated southern segment of the multi-purpose hiking, biking and equestrian trail. The trail meanders along the Salinas River through riparian vegetation with stands of oaks, sycamores, cottonwoods and willows.

Driving directions: From Highway 101 in Atascadero, exit on Curbaril Avenue and drive 1.1 mile east to Garbada Road, the first road after crossing the railroad tracks. Turn right and drive 0.2 miles to Tampico Road—turn left. Continue 0.2 miles to Aragon Road. Turn right and park on the left in the Wranglerette Arena parking area. The trailhead is on Aragon Road at the end of the block.

Hiking directions: Walk to the end of Aragon Road and through the opening in the brush. Take the well-defined path a hundred yards to a trail split. The left fork leads 0.3 miles downstream, dropping into a sandy streambed and ending at the river's edge. The right fork bears south 0.2 miles to another junction. These two trails parallel each other and intertwine with numerous connector trails. Both trails meander upstream between the disposal ponds on the west and the Salinas River on the east. Side paths lead to the river's edge. At 0.8 miles, the trail drops into a sandy creekbed between two ranches. This is a good turnaround spot.

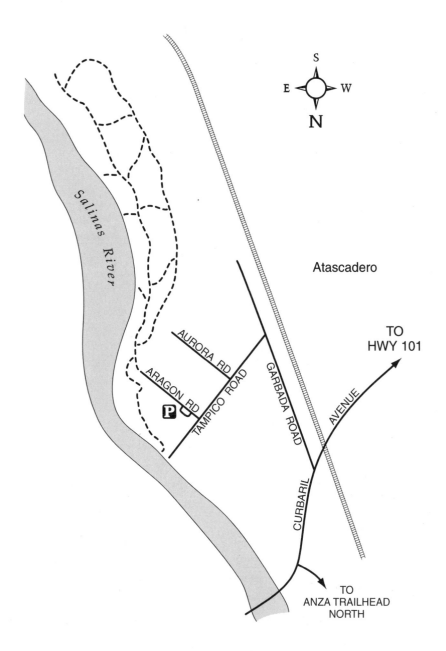

ANZA NATIONAL HISTORIC TRAIL–SOUTH

Hike 13
Jim Green Trail
Heilman Regional Park

Hiking distance: 1.5 mile loop
Hiking time: 1 hour
Elevation gain: 200 feet
Maps: U.S.G.S. Atascadero
The Thomas Guide—San Luis Obispo County

Summary of hike: Heilman Regional Park encompasses 315 acres with equestrian and hiking trails. The Jim Green Trail is accessed from the northern end of the park. The trail loops around the contours of the hillsides to scenic overlooks of Chalk Mountain Golf Course, the Salinas River and the surrounding mountains. The path weaves through groves of oak trees draped with strands of hanging moss.

Driving directions: From Highway 101 in Atascadero, exit on Curbaril Avenue, and drive one mile east to Cortez Avenue. Turn right and drive 0.2 miles to the parking lot on the left at the end of the road.

Hiking directions: Hike south past the trail sign between the railroad tracks and the pole-rail fence to a trail fork. The right fork is the return path. Continue straight ahead to a second trail split. The left fork continues parallel to the railroad tracks and ends at the golf course a short distance ahead. Take the right fork, gaining elevation across the oak-covered grassy hillside. At the ridge is a bench overlooking the surrounding mountains, the golf course and the disposal ponds. The trail loops back along the ridge and descends through the forest, completing the loop. Bear to the left, returning to the trailhead.

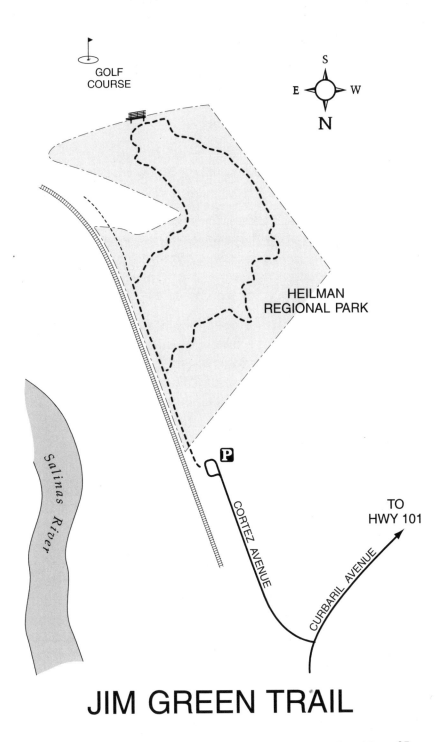

GOLF
COURSE

S
E · W
N

HEILMAN
REGIONAL PARK

Salinas River

P

TO
HWY 101

CORTEZ AVENUE

CURBARIL AVENUE

JIM GREEN TRAIL

Hike 14
Cerro Alto Loop Trail

Hiking distance: 2.5 mile loop
Hiking time: 1.5 hours
Elevation gain: 640 feet
Maps: U.S.G.S. Atascadero
      The Mountain Biking Map for San Luis Obispo

Summary of hike: For those who wish to enjoy the Cerro Alto area without climbing 1,600 feet to the peak, the Cerro Alto Loop Trail is perfect. The trail parallels the upper East Fork of Morro Creek up a lush narrow canyon with oaks, sycamores and cottonwoods. The hike traverses the mountain slopes to various overlooks, then descends into an oak woodland.

Driving directions: The trail is located between Morro Bay and Atascadero. From Highway 101 in Atascadero, take the Highway 41 West/Morro Bay exit, and head 8.7 miles west to the Cerro Alto Campground turnoff. Turn left and continue 0.9 miles up the winding road to the parking lot at the end of the road. A parking fee is required.
    From Highway 1 in Morro Bay, head 7.2 miles east on Highway 41 to the campground turnoff on the right.

Hiking directions: From the east end of the parking area by campsite 19, take the signed Cerro Alto Trail. Traverse up the north wall of the canyon through an oak forest above the fern-lined creek. Cross the creekbed, continuing to the head of the canyon. At 0.8 miles is a signed junction. Go right towards the summit, bearing right past two intersecting trails on the left to an overlook above the canyon. Heading west, follow the contours of Cerro Alto Mountain to overlooks of Morro Bay. At 1.5 miles is a junction with the trail to the summit (Hike 15). Stay to the right, heading downhill to a signed junction 200 yards ahead. Bear right, down the hillside. Switchbacks lead into a live oak forest. Cross the bridge over the East Fork of Morro Creek, returning to the campground by the parking lot.

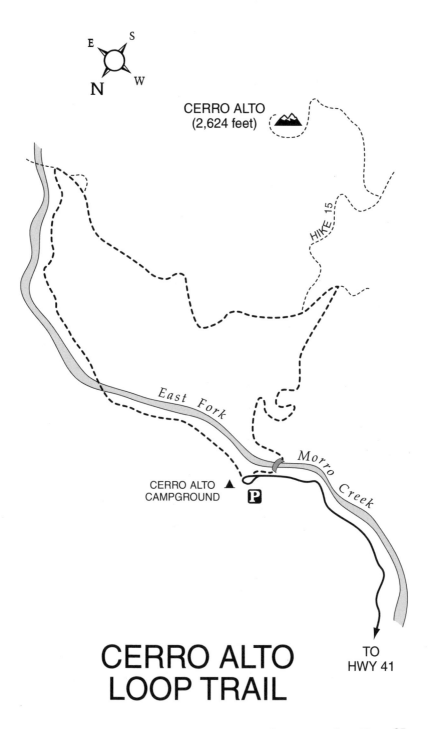

E S

N W

CERRO ALTO
(2,624 feet)

HIKE 15

East Fork

Morro Creek

CERRO ALTO ▲
CAMPGROUND P

CERRO ALTO
LOOP TRAIL

TO
HWY 41

Hike 15
Cerro Alto Summit

Hiking distance: 4 miles round trip
Hiking time: 2.5 hours
Elevation gain: 1,650 feet
Maps: U.S.G.S. Atascadero
         The Mountain Biking Map for San Luis Obispo

Summary of hike: At 2,624 feet, the Cerro Alto summit has spectacular, unlimited 360-degree views of the central coast's beautiful landscape. The peak overlooks Morro Rock, Morro Bay and the Pacific Ocean to the west; Cambria, San Simeon and the Piedras Blancas Lighthouse to the northwest; and Cuesta Ridge, San Luis Obispo and the Santa Lucia Mountains to the southeast.

Driving directions: The trail is located between Morro Bay and Atascadero. From Highway 101 in Atascadero, take the Highway 41 West/Morro Bay exit, and head 8.7 miles west to the Cerro Alto Campground turnoff. Turn left and continue 0.9 miles up the winding road to the parking lot at the end of the road. A parking fee is required.

From Highway 1 in Morro Bay, head 7.2 miles east on Highway 41 to the campground turnoff on the right.

Hiking directions: From the parking area, return back down the road 20 yards to the signed trail on the left by campsite 16. Descend into a forest of bays and live oaks, then cross a wooden bridge over the East Fork of Morro Creek. Switchbacks lead through the forest onto the chaparral-covered hillside. Continue up the drainage to a signed junction with a fire road at 0.7 miles. Bear left for 200 yards uphill to a signed junction on the right with the Cerro Alto Trail to the summit. The trail curves along the edge of the mountainside, crossing two drainages to an unsigned junction. Bear left, circling the peak up to the summit. After resting and marveling at the views, return by retracing your steps.

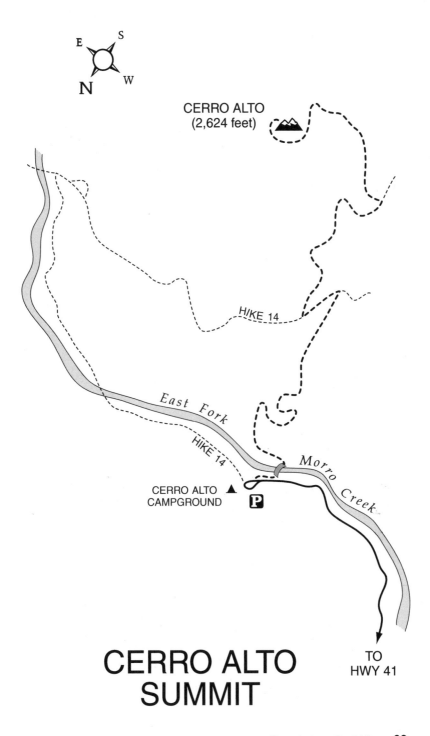

E **S**
N **W**

CERRO ALTO
(2,624 feet)

HIKE 14

East Fork

HIKE 14

Morro Creek

CERRO ALTO ▲
CAMPGROUND
P

CERRO ALTO
SUMMIT

TO
HWY 41

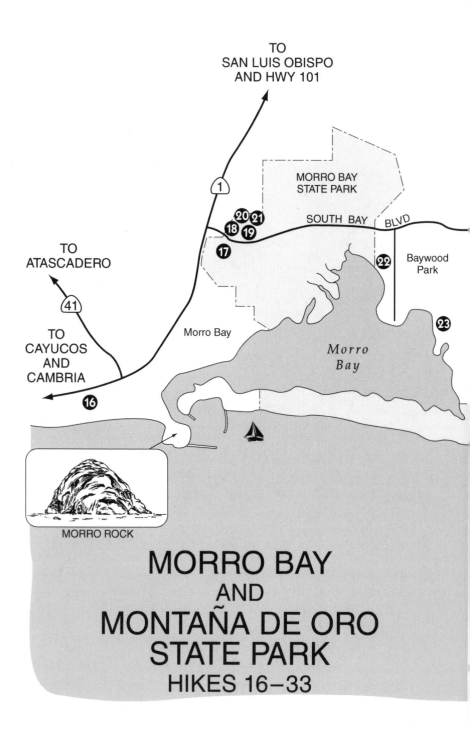

TO
SAN LUIS OBISPO
AND HWY 101

MORRO BAY
STATE PARK

SOUTH BAY BLVD

TO
ATASCADERO

TO
CAYUCOS
AND
CAMBRIA

Morro Bay

*Morro
Bay*

Baywood
Park

MORRO ROCK

MORRO BAY
AND
MONTAÑA DE ORO
STATE PARK
HIKES 16–33

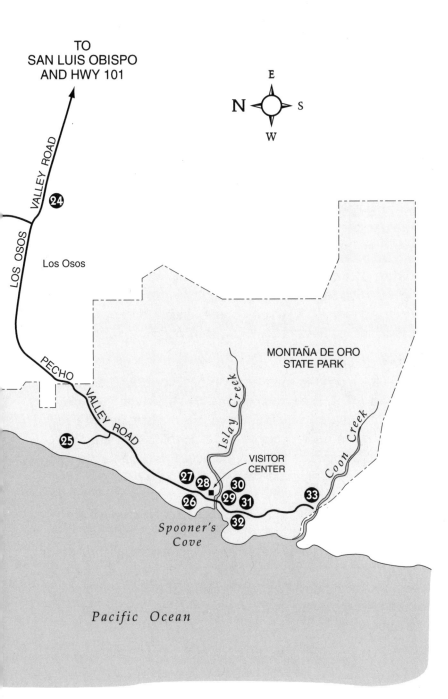

TO
SAN LUIS OBISPO
AND HWY 101

N E S W

VALLEY ROAD

LOS OSOS

24

Los Osos

PECHO VALLEY ROAD

MONTAÑA DE ORO
STATE PARK

Islay Creek

Coon Creek

VISITOR
CENTER

25

27
28
26
30
29 31
32
33

Spooner's
Cove

Pacific Ocean

Hike 16
Cloisters Wetland to Morro Rock

Hiking distance: 3.5 miles round trip
Hiking time: 1.5 hours
Elevation gain: Level
Maps: U.S.G.S. Morro Bay North and Morro Bay South

Summary of hike: The Cloisters Wetland is a 2.6-acre wildlife habitat with a freshwater lagoon. A trail with interpretive signs circles the lagoon. The hike crosses Morro Strand State Beach to Morro Rock, a dome-shaped volcanic plug rising from the ocean at the mouth of the harbor. This ancient 578-foot monolithic outcropping is a wildlife preserve.

Driving directions: From Highway 1 in Morro Bay, head 2 miles north to San Jacinto Street and turn left. Drive to the first street and turn left again on Coral Avenue. Continue 0.3 miles and park in the Cloisters Community Park parking lot on the right.

Hiking directions: Take the paved path through the developed park along the south side of the lagoon. At the dunes is a junction. The right fork circles the Cloisters Wetland, a freshwater lagoon. Bear left and follow the path between the dunes and the park meadow towards the prominent Morro Rock. The trail curves through the dunes, crossing a wooden footbridge. Bear right and walk parallel to a row of pine trees to the end of the boardwalk at the sandy beach. Follow the shoreline of Morro Strand State Beach directly towards Morro Rock. Cross the sand isthmus to the base of the rock. Walk across the parking area and follow Coleman Drive (the paved road) clockwise around the perimeter of Morro Rock along the edge of the bay. At the west end of the rock is a sandy beach and breakwater at the entrance to the bay. Return along the same route.

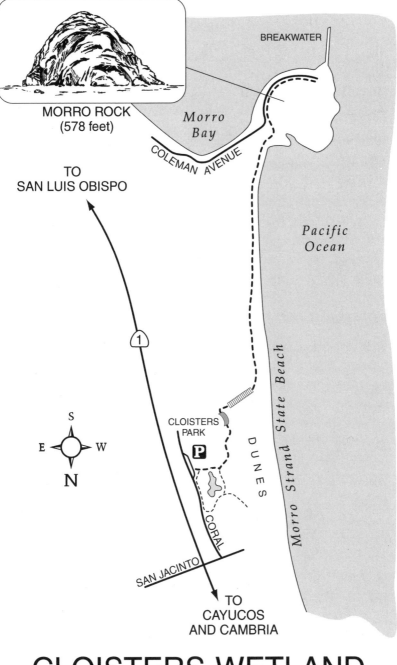

MORRO ROCK
(578 feet)

BREAKWATER

Morro Bay

COLEMAN AVENUE

Pacific Ocean

TO
SAN LUIS OBISPO

1

CLOISTERS
PARK

P

DUNES

Morro Strand State Beach

CORAL

SAN JACINTO

TO
CAYUCOS
AND CAMBRIA

S
E — W
N

CLOISTERS WETLAND

Hike 17
Black Hill
Morro Bay State Park

Hiking distance: 0.6—2.6 miles round trip
Hiking time: 30 minutes—1.5 hours
Elevation gain: 180—540 feet
Maps: U.S.G.S. Morro Bay South

Summary of hike: Black Hill (also known an Black Mountain) is an ancient 661-foot volcanic peak in Morro Bay State Park. There is a short easy trail to the rocky summit and a longer forested route. The longer route climbs through the shade of a eucalyptus forest, an oak woodland and Monterey pine groves. From the rocky summit are panoramic views of Morro Bay and the estuary, Estero Point, Cayucos, Chorro Valley, and the nearby morros of Cerro Cabrillo and Hollister Peak. The ocean views span from Montaña de Oro to San Simeon.

Driving directions: From Highway 101 south of San Luis Obispo, take the Los Osos Valley Road exit, and head 9.6 miles west to South Bay Road. Turn right and continue 3.2 miles to State Park Road and turn left.

From Highway 1 in Morro Bay, head 0.8 miles south on South Bay Boulevard to State Park Road and turn right.

FOR THE LONG HIKE, bear right 0.1 mile ahead at a road fork and head up Park View Drive for 0.3 miles to a parking pullout on the left.

FOR THE SHORT HIKE, bear right 0.1 mile ahead at a road fork and head 0.6 miles up Park View Drive to the unsigned Black Mountain Road and turn right. Continue 0.7 miles through the golf course to the trailhead parking area at the end of the road.

Hiking directions: For the long hike, walk 100 yards up the road to the trail on the right with the "no bikes" sign. Head north across a meadow, dropping into a ravine to a T-junction. Bear left through a eucalyptus grove past an intersecting trail on the right. A short distance ahead is a third junction. Bear right, gaining elevation through an oak woodland. At one mile, loop around the right side of a cement water tank to the upper trailhead parking lot. This is where the short hike begins. Head northeast up several switchbacks to the summit. After marveling at the views, return by retracing your steps.

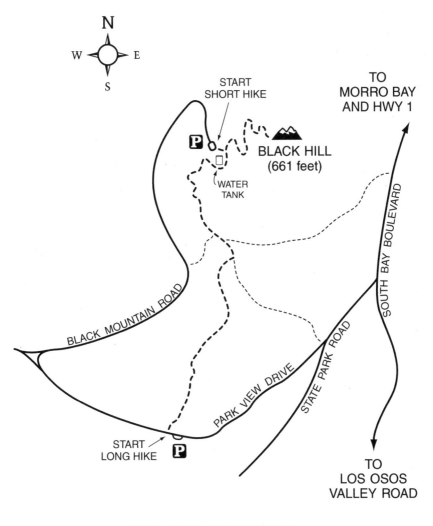

BLACK HILL

Hike 18
Chorro Hill
Morro Bay State Park

Hiking distance: 1.8 miles round trip
Hiking time: 1 hour
Elevation gain: 200 feet
Maps: U.S.G.S. Morro Bay South

Summary of hike: Chorro Hill (also known as Turtle Rock) is a 209-foot rounded outcropping in Morro Bay State Park. The rocky hill sits to the east of Black Hill (Hike 17) and at the northwest base of Cerro Cabrillo. Monterey pines grow around the rocky peak. The summit overlooks the four-mile expanse of Morro Bay and the estuary, a bird and wildlife habitat where the fresh water of Chorro Creek and Los Osos Creek mix with the salt water of the ocean.

Driving directions: From Highway 101 south of San Luis Obispo, take the Los Osos Valley Road exit, and head 9.6 miles west to South Bay Road. Turn right and continue 2.6 miles to the trailhead parking lot on the right.

From Highway 1 in Morro Bay, head 1.4 miles south on South Bay Boulevard to the trailhead parking lot on the left.

Hiking directions: Take the signed Quarry Trail east up the scrubby slope. At 200 yards is a trail on the left. Bear left, heading around the lower west slope of Cerro Cabrillo above South Bay Road. Notice the marbled effect of the streams meandering through the Morro Bay estuary. Once around the western flank of Cerro Cabrillo, descend to a fenced service road. Veer to the right, following the road up to Chorro Hill. At the top of the road is a locked gate and fenceline at the park boundary. Take the footpath to the left, winding up to the rocky summit. The final ascent curves around large boulders to the Monterey pines at the summit. After enjoying the views, return the way you came.

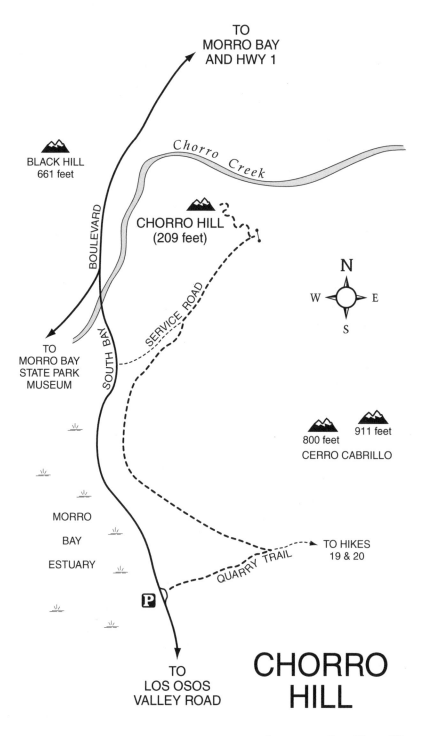

TO
MORRO BAY
AND HWY 1

Chorro Creek

BLACK HILL
661 feet

BOULEVARD

CHORRO HILL
(209 feet)

SOUTH BAY

SERVICE ROAD

TO
MORRO BAY
STATE PARK
MUSEUM

N
W ⊕ E
S

911 feet
800 feet
CERRO CABRILLO

MORRO

BAY

ESTUARY

TO HIKES
19 & 20

QUARRY TRAIL

P

TO
LOS OSOS
VALLEY ROAD

CHORRO
HILL

Hike 19
Portola Point
Morro Bay State Park

Hiking distance: 2 miles round trip
Hiking time: 1 hour
Elevation gain: 320 feet
Maps: U.S.G.S. Morro Bay South
      The Mountain Biking Map for San Luis Obispo

Summary of hike: Portola Hill is a 329-foot rounded volcanic hill on the east side of Morro Bay State Park. A spur trail leads up to Portola Point, offering sweeping views of the surrounding morros and the Morro Bay area, one of the most vital and productive bird habitats in the country. The hike follows the Quarry and Live Oak Trails across rolling native grassland, looping around the base of Portola Hill.

Driving directions: From Highway 101 south of San Luis Obispo, take the Los Osos Valley Road exit, and head 9.6 miles west to South Bay Road. Turn right and continue 2.6 miles to the trailhead parking lot on the right.
From Highway 1 in Morro Bay, head 1.4 miles south on South Bay Boulevard to the trailhead parking lot on the left.

Hiking directions: Take the signed Quarry Trail uphill through the sage scrub. Head east along the south facing slopes of Cerro Cabrillo to a signed junction at 0.5 miles. Take the Live Oak Trail to the right, descending across a grassy meadow towards Portola Hill. Near the base of the hill is a signed trail fork. Bear right on the Portola Trail, and ascend the hill past an oak grove. Switchbacks lead up to a trail split, circling the point to various overlooks and a resting bench. Complete the loop and return to the Live Oak Trail. Go right and descend into the draw between Portola Hill and Hill 811. At 1.5 miles is a signed trail split. Bear right, contouring around Portola Hill on the Live Oak Trail. Return to the parking lot.

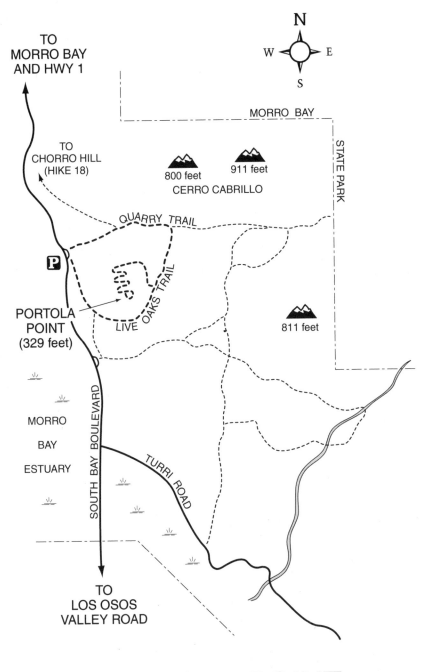

TO
MORRO BAY
AND HWY 1

N

W ⬥ E

S

MORRO BAY

TO
CHORRO HILL
(HIKE 18)

STATE PARK

800 feet   911 feet
CERRO CABRILLO

QUARRY TRAIL

P

LIVE OAKS TRAIL

811 feet

PORTOLA
POINT
(329 feet)

MORRO

BAY

ESTUARY

SOUTH BAY BOULEVARD

TURRI ROAD

TO
LOS OSOS
VALLEY ROAD

PORTOLA POINT

Hike 20
Quarry and Park Ridge Loop Trail
Morro Bay State Park

Hiking distance: 2.5 miles round trip
Hiking time: 1 hour
Elevation gain: 350 feet
Maps: U.S.G.S. Morro Bay South
The Mountain Biking Map for San Luis Obispo

Summary of hike: The Quarry and Park Ridge Trails are on the east side of Morro Bay State Park under the shadow of Cerro Cabrillo, a 911-foot double-peaked ridge. The Quarry Trail skirts the southern flank of Cerro Cabrillo past the rubble piles of an abandoned quarry site used for road construction in 1959. The Park Ridge Trail is an old farm road that crosses the rolling grasslands.

Driving directions: From Highway 101 south of San Luis Obispo, take the Los Osos Valley Road exit, and head 9.6 miles west to South Bay Road. Turn right and continue 2.6 miles to the trailhead parking lot on the right.
From Highway 1 in Morro Bay, head 1.4 miles south on South Bay Boulevard to the trailhead parking lot on the left.

Hiking directions: Take the signed Quarry Trail toward the foot of Cerro Cabrillo. The trail parallels the base of the mountain, passing the quarry site on the left. Continue past the Live Oak Trail on the right (Hike 19) to a junction at 0.9 miles with the Park Ridge Trail on the right. Stay on the Quarry Trail, heading east to the signed junction with the Canet Trail on the right. The Quarry Trail ends 0.2 miles ahead at the fenced park boundary. Take the Canet Trail south, crossing the rolling hill to a saddle and a junction. Bear left on the Park Ridge Trail, and head downhill to a trail split with the Chumash Trail. Veer right and stay right again at a junction with the Crespi Trail (Hike 21). Cross a small bridge, returning to a gate near South Bay Road. Bear right (north) on the Live Oak Trail back to the parking lot.

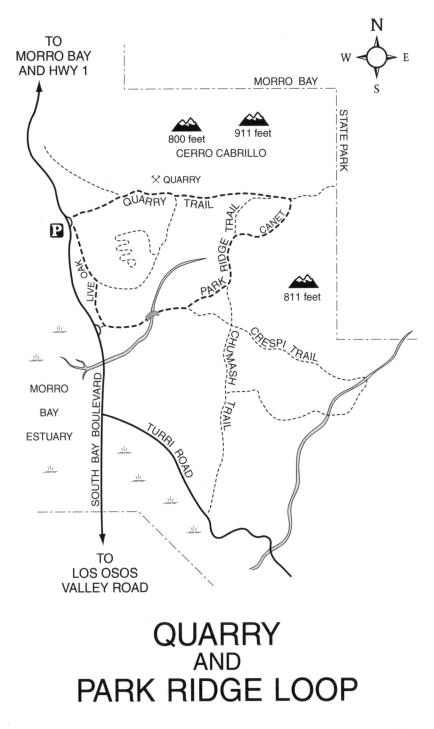

QUARRY
AND
PARK RIDGE LOOP

Hike 21
Crespi Trail
Morro Bay State Park

Hiking distance: 3.2 miles round trip
Hiking time: 1.5 hours
Elevation gain: 300 feet
Maps: U.S.G.S. Morro Bay South
       The Mountain Biking Map For San Luis Obispo

Summary of hike: The Crespi Trail is in the eastern portion of Morro Bay State Park south of Cerro Cabrillo. The trail winds across the hills through coastal sage scrub and pockets of coastal live oak. There are great views of the Morro Bay estuary to the west and Hollister Peak to the east. The verdant rolling grasslands were once part of the Baptista and Pedro Ranches.

Driving directions: From Highway 101 south of San Luis Obispo, take the Los Osos Valley Road exit, and head 9.6 miles west to South Bay Road. Turn right and continue 2.2 miles to the trailhead parking area on the right.
    From Highway 1 in Morro Bay, head 1.8 miles south on South Bay Boulevard to the trailhead parking area on the left.

Hiking directions: Head east on the Park Ridge Trail across the rolling grasslands and cross a seasonal streambed. Continue past a large outcropping on the left to a signed trail split at 0.3 miles. The left fork is the Park Ridge Trail (Hike 20). Bear right on the Crespi Trail to a four-way junction with the Chumash Trail at 0.5 miles. Continue straight ahead, staying on the Crespi Trail along the hillside to a saddle. Descend into the drainage to a canopy of coastal live oak. Cross the creek and curve to the right down the drainage. Return up the hillside, curving west to a junction. Bear right on the Chumash Trail, completing the loop at a junction with the Crespi Trail. Go left and return to the trailhead.

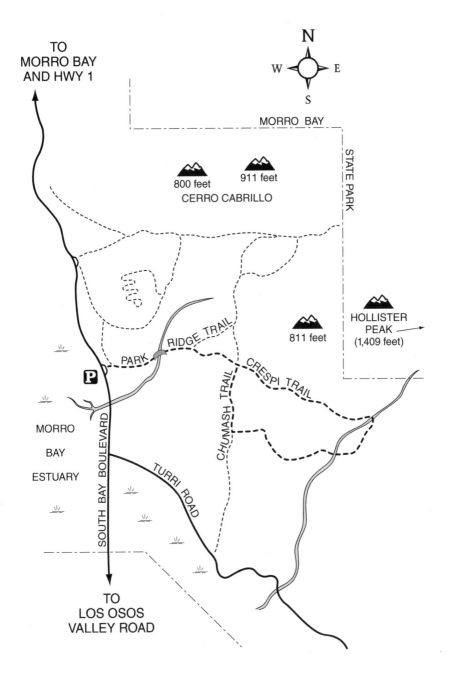

CRESPI TRAIL

Hike 22
Elfin Forest Natural Area

Hiking distance: 1.5 miles round trip
Hiking time: 1 hour
Elevation gain: 100 feet
Maps: U.S.G.S. Morro Bay South

Summary of hike: The Elfin Forest Natural Area is a 92-acre refuge at the eastern shore of Morro Bay abutting the estuary. A mile of wooden walkways with viewing platforms and overlooks form an oval loop around the forest. The area includes a salt marsh, coastal dune scrub, morro manzanita, riparian woodland and dense stands of dwarfed 500-year-old pygmy oaks. The gnarled, windswept oaks have room-like openings and are draped with moss and lichens.

Driving directions: From Highway 101 south of San Luis Obispo, take the Los Osos Valley Road exit, and head 9.6 miles west to South Bay Road. Turn right and continue 1.4 miles to Santa Ysabel Avenue on the left. Turn left and drive to 16th Street. Turn right and park at the end of the block.
   From Highway 1 in Morro Bay, head 2.7 miles south on South Bay Boulevard to Santa Ysabel Avenue. Turn right and follow the directions above.

Hiking directions: Head north at the end of 16th Street on the wooden boardwalk. Walk through the dense sage scrub to the ridge overlooking the Morro Bay estuary. Bear left (west), following the Ridge Trail boardwalk to an overlook at the west end. A sandy path returns to 11th and 13th Streets. From the overlook, return east 150 yards to a junction and bear left. Descend to the Celestial Meadow Trail. The left fork leads to another overlook platform at the edge of the estuary. The right fork heads uphill to a junction with the Ridge Trail. Here the left fork leads to a third viewing platform. The right fork completes the loop on the ridge by 16th Street.

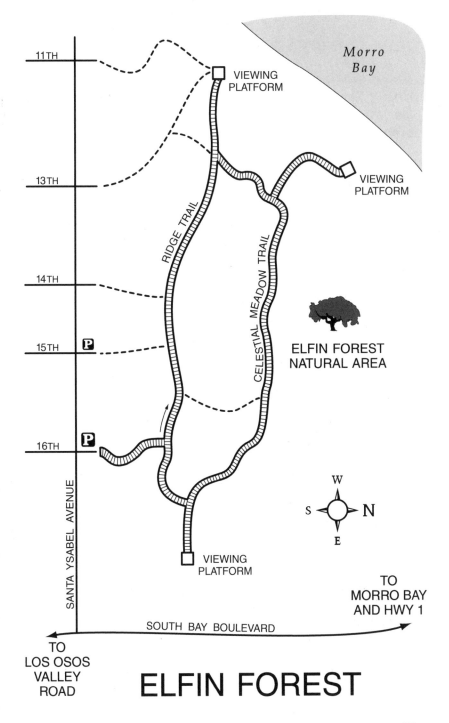

ELFIN FOREST

Hike 23
Sweet Springs Nature Preserve

Hiking distance: 0.5 to 1 mile round trip
Hiking time: 30 minutes
Elevation gain: Level
Maps: U.S.G.S. Morro Bay South

Summary of hike: Sweet Springs Nature Preserve is a 24-acre wetland sanctuary for nesting and migrating birds on the southeast shore of Morro Bay. There are two serene freshwater ponds, a saltwater marsh at the bay, Monterey cypress and eucalyptus groves. The eucalyptus groves are home to monarch butterflies during the winter months. The preserve is managed by the Morro Coast Audubon Society

Driving directions: From Highway 101 south of San Luis Obispo, take the Los Osos Valley Road exit, and head 10.1 miles west to 9th Street (0.5 miles past South Bay Boulevard). Turn right and drive 0.6 miles to Ramona Avenue, curving to the left. Continue 0.5 miles to the nature preserve on the right. Park along the road.

From Highway 1 in Morro Bay, head 4 miles south on South Bay Boulevard to Los Osos Valley Road and turn right. Continue 0.5 miles to 9th Street and turn right. Follow directions above.

Hiking directions: From the preserve entrance gate, walk past the trail sign and cross a wooden footbridge over the pond. Bear left to a second wooden bridge. Towards the right is a maze of waterways winding through the estuary. After crossing the bridge, the trail weaves through a eucalyptus grove. At the west end of the preserve is a junction. The left fork returns to the road at Broderson Street. The right fork leads to an overlook of the bay and marshy tidelands. Morro Rock can be seen at the north end of the bay. Return to the first bridge. Bear to the left, heading east alongside the pond. The trail loops back through another eucalyptus grove and returns to the park entrance.

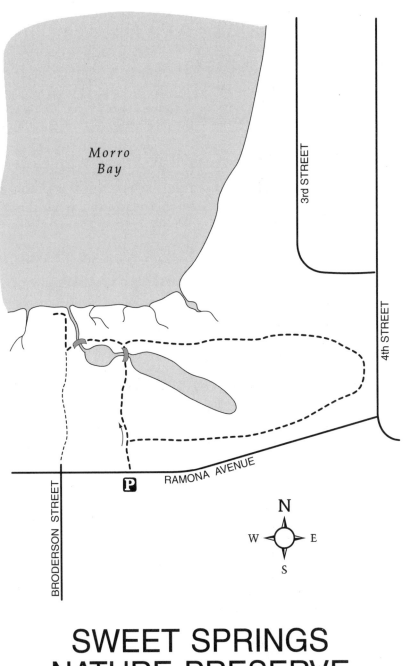

Morro Bay

3rd STREET

4th STREET

RAMONA AVENUE

BRODERSON STREET

P

N
W   E
S

SWEET SPRINGS
NATURE PRESERVE

Hike 24
Los Osos Oaks State Reserve

Hiking distance: 2 miles round trip
Hiking time: 1 hour
Elevation gain: 100 feet
Maps: U.S.G.S. Morro Bay South

Summary of hike: Los Osos Oaks State Reserve encompasses 85 acres that was once home to the Chumash Indians. This small reserve has ancient stands of 600- to 800-year-old dwarfed oaks. Lace lichen streamers hang from the massive, twisted and contorted branches. Three short, enchanting loop trails meander under the canopy of these unique old growth oaks past ferns, mushrooms and poison oak. Los Osos Creek follows the eastern edge of the preserve under the shade of sycamore, willow, laurel and cottonwood trees.

Driving directions: From Highway 101 south of San Luis Obispo, take the Los Osos Valley Road exit, and head 8.9 miles west to the signed trailhead parking lot on the left.

From Highway 1 in Morro Bay, head 4 miles south on South Bay Boulevard to Los Osos Valley Road and turn left. Drive 0.7 miles to the signed trailhead parking lot on the right.

Hiking directions: Head south on the signed trail under the dense forest canopy of coastal live oaks. Cross a wooden bridge over the trickling feeder stream to a four-way junction. All three trails loop back, returning to this junction. To the left is the Los Osos Creek Trail; to the right is the Chumash Loop Trail; and straight ahead is the Oak View Trail. The left fork loops around the east border of the park above the perennial Los Osos Creek. It leads into grasslands and native chaparral to an overlook of Los Osos Valley, the Irish Hills and the Santa Lucia Mountains. Various side paths lead left to creekside overlooks. The trail loops back, reentering the dense forest to junctions with the other two trails. Stroll through the shady reserve on the well-defined trails, choosing your own path.

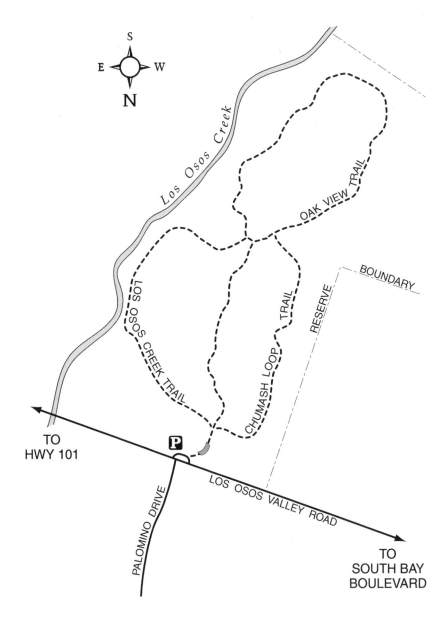

S

E ☀ W

N

Los Osos Creek

OAK VIEW TRAIL

BOUNDARY

RESERVE

LOS OSOS CREEK TRAIL

CHUMASH LOOP TRAIL

TO
HWY 101

P

PALOMINO DRIVE

LOS OSOS VALLEY ROAD

TO
SOUTH BAY
BOULEVARD

LOS OSOS OAKS
STATE RESERVE

Hike 25
Morro Bay Sand Spit
Montaña de Oro State Park

Hiking distance: 8 to 9.5 miles round trip
Hiking time: 3 to 5 hours
Elevation gain: 50 feet
Maps: U.S.G.S. Morro Bay South
Montaña de Oro State Park map

Summary of hike: The Morro Bay Sand Spit is three-mile long narrow vein of land that separates Morro Bay and the estuary from the waters of Estero Bay and the Pacific Ocean. A fragile 80-foot sand dune ridge, stabilized by scrubs, grasses and succulents, runs the length of this natural preserve. Along the dunes are ancient Chumash Indian shell mounds. This hike follows the sand spit along the ocean side of the dunes.

Driving directions: From Highway 101 south of San Luis Obispo, take the Los Osos Valley Road exit, and head 12.1 miles west to the Montaña de Oro State Park entrance. Los Osos Valley Road becomes Pecho Valley Road en route. Continue 0.8 miles to Sand Spit Road and turn right. Drive 0.5 miles to the parking lot at the end of the road.

Hiking directions: Take the lined path past the information boards and head west across the scrub-covered sand dunes. The path reaches the ocean at 0.2 miles. Head north along the hard-packed sand close to the shoreline for easier walking. The coastline has an abundance of sea shells. At 4 miles is the first of two breakwaters guarding the bay entrance. Morro Rock, a 578-foot volcanic rock, dominates the landscape. This is a good turnaround spot. To add an additional 1.5 miles to the hike, continue following the shoreline to a second breakwater. Curve east towards Morro Bay, and follow the bay south about one mile. The trail curves west, crossing the soft sands of the dunes back to the ocean.

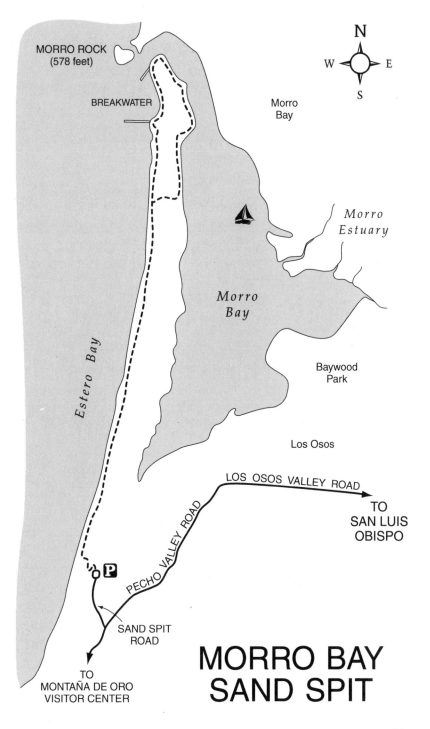

MORRO ROCK
(578 feet)

BREAKWATER

Morro
Bay

*Morro
Estuary*

*Morro
Bay*

Estero Bay

Baywood
Park

Los Osos

LOS OSOS VALLEY ROAD

TO
SAN LUIS
OBISPO

PECHO VALLEY ROAD

P

SAND SPIT
ROAD

TO
MONTAÑA DE ORO
VISITOR CENTER

MORRO BAY
SAND SPIT

Hike 26
Dunes Trail to Hazard Canyon Reef
Montaña de Oro State Park

Hiking distance: 2.6 miles round trip
Hiking time: 1.5 hours
Elevation gain: 50 feet
Maps: U.S.G.S. Morro Bay South
       Montaña de Oro State Park map

Summary of hike: The Dunes Trail parallels the ocean bluffs across scrub-covered dunes from Spooner's Cove. The trail leads down narrow Hazard Canyon in a eucalyptus grove to Hazard Canyon Reef, a rocky beach cove with superb tidepools at the base of the cliffs. Above Hazard Canyon Reef is a stunning overlook of the scalloped coastline.

Driving directions: From Highway 101 south of San Luis Obispo, take the Los Osos Valley Road exit, and head 12.1 miles west to the Montaña de Oro State Park entrance. Los Osos Valley Road becomes Pecho Valley Road en route. Continue 2.5 miles to the trailhead parking area on the right, just north of Spooner's Cove. The visitor center is 0.1 mile ahead on the left.

Hiking directions: At the signed trailhead are two trails. The left fork is a loop that curves around Spooner's Cove and the bluffs before reconnecting with the Dunes Trail a short distance ahead. The right fork is the Dunes Trail, heading north across the scrub-covered sand dunes. The sandy trail parallels the coastline between the bluffs and Pecho Valley Road. At 0.5 miles, the trail crosses a junction. To the right is a parking area by the park road. The left route heads across the rolling dunes to a surfing beach. Continue straight ahead to a trail split at one mile. Bear right to a parking area in a eucalyptus grove. Pick up the trail again on the left. Long, wide steps descend into narrow Hazard Canyon. Cross a wooden boardwalk alongside a small creek to Hazard Canyon Reef, another surfing beach. This is a great spot for beachcombing and enjoying the tidepools along the base of the cliffs. The Hazard Reef Trail heads up to the bluffs to an overlook of the rugged coastline. This is the turnaround spot. Return along the same path.

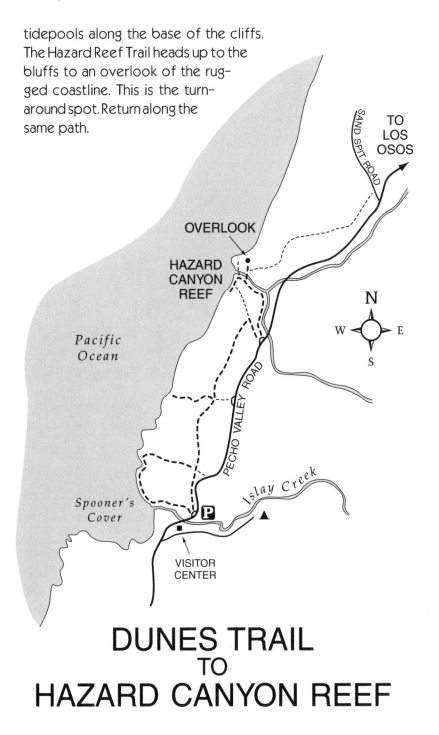

DUNES TRAIL
TO
HAZARD CANYON REEF

Hike 27
Ridge Trail to Hazard Peak
Montaña de Oro State Park

Hiking distance: 4.6 miles round trip
Hiking time: 2 hours
Elevation gain: 1,000 feet
Maps: U.S.G.S. Morro Bay South
Montaña de Oro State Park map

Summary of hike: The Ridge Trail crosses the shoulder of the mountain to Hazard Peak, a 1,076-foot grassy summit. The trail follows the ridge east while overlooking Islay Creek, Spooner Cove, the bluffs and the dunes. The hike ends at an overlook just beyond Hazard Peak. From the overlook are views into Hazard Canyon and across the sand spit to Morro Rock and the bay.

Driving directions: From Highway 101 south of San Luis Obispo, take the Los Osos Valley Road exit, and head 12.1 miles west to the Montaña de Oro State Park entrance. Los Osos Valley Road becomes Pecho Valley Road en route. Continue 2.3 miles to the signed trailhead on the left. There are parking areas on both sides of the road. The visitor center is 0.3 miles ahead.

Hiking directions: Hike east past the trail sign on the wide path. Cross the rolling foothills through a dense thicket of scrubs up to a ridge. Curve north, then east up the hillside towards a large rounded hill. The trail traverses the hillside to the right, 600 feet above Islay Canyon. Continue ascending the hill to a saddle. At 2.2 miles, a ridge leads to Hazard Peak on the left. From Hazard Peak, follow the narrow ridge between two steep drainages to an overlook at a fenceline and survey pin. Although the trail continues to connecting trails into Hazard Canyon and Islay Canyon, this is the turnaround spot.

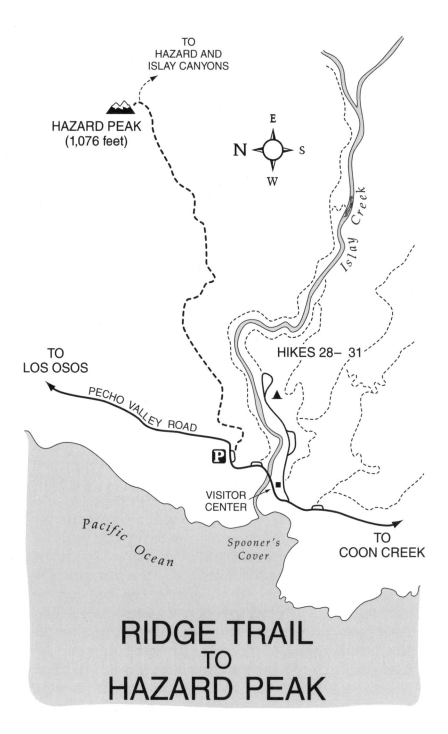

TO
HAZARD AND
ISLAY CANYONS

HAZARD PEAK
(1,076 feet)

N E S W

Islay Creek

HIKES 28– 31

TO
LOS OSOS

PECHO VALLEY ROAD

P

VISITOR
CENTER

TO
COON CREEK

Pacific Ocean

Spooner's Cover

RIDGE TRAIL
TO
HAZARD PEAK

Hike 28
Islay Creek Trail
Montaña de Oro State Park

Hiking distance: 6 miles round trip
Hiking time: 3 hours
Elevation gain: 300 feet
Maps: U.S.G.S. Morro Bay South
       Montaña de Oro State Park map

Summary of hike: The Islay Creek Trail follows an old ranch road up the north side of Islay Canyon parallel to Islay Creek. The wide, level trail passes a waterfall to an old abandoned barn in the mountainous interior of the canyon.

Driving directions: From Highway 101 south of San Luis Obispo, take the Los Osos Valley Road exit, and head 12.1 miles west to the Montaña de Oro State Park entrance. Los Osos Valley Road becomes Pecho Valley Road en route. Continue 2.4 miles to the trailhead parking area on the left by the signed trailhead. The visitor center is 0.2 miles ahead.

Hiking directions: Hike past the metal gate on the unpaved ranch road. The road winds along the south-facing hillside above Islay Creek and the campground. At a quarter mile, weathered Monterey shale forms a beautiful rock wall along the cliff side of the trail. At one mile is a signed junction with the Reservoir Flats Trail on the right (Hike 29). This short detour descends 50 yards down to the creek. Back on the main trail, continue to a narrow unsigned trail on the right at 1.3 miles. This footpath leads down the steep cliff to a waterfall. This scramble is not easy, and the waterfall can be seen from the main trail before reaching the footpath. At two miles, Islay Creek forks. Just beyond the fork is a signed junction with the South Fork Islay Trail, a loop trail to the right. Follow the main road, passing the Barranca Trail on the left. Cross a bridge to the old barn at 2.9 miles. The Islay Creek Trail ends at the gated eastern border of the park. Return the way you came.

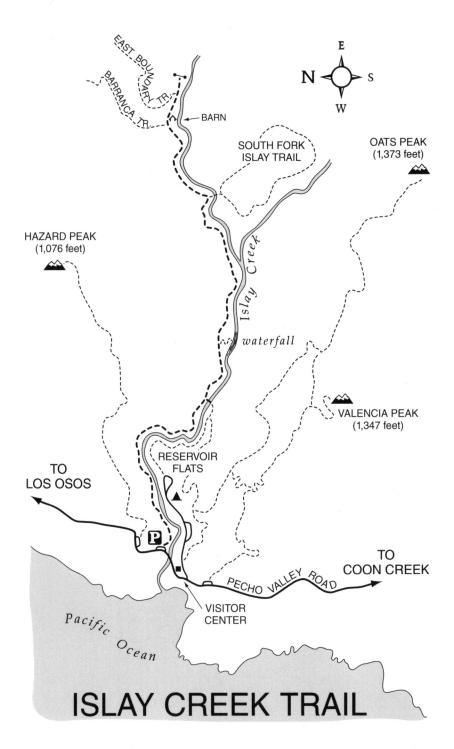

EAST BOUNDARY TR.

BARRANCA TR.

BARN

SOUTH FORK
ISLAY TRAIL

OATS PEAK
(1,373 feet)

N

E

S

W

HAZARD PEAK
(1,076 feet)

Islay Creek

waterfall

VALENCIA PEAK
(1,347 feet)

RESERVOIR
FLATS

TO
LOS OSOS

P

TO
COON CREEK

PECHO VALLEY ROAD

VISITOR
CENTER

Pacific
Ocean

ISLAY CREEK TRAIL

Hike 29
Reservoir Flats Trail
Montaña de Oro State Park

Hiking distance: 2.1 mile loop
Hiking time: 1 hour
Elevation gain: 250 feet
Maps: U.S.G.S. Morro Bay South
       Montaña de Oro State Park map

Summary of hike: The Reservoir Flats Trail follows a creekside canyon parallel to Islay Creek. Ferns and moss carpet the lush canyon, willows line the creek, and lichen streamers hang from the branches of the trees. After leaving the canyon, the trail reaches a ridge along the grassy hillside to the former reservoir site. From the ridge are views of Islay Canyon, the bluffs, Spooner's Cove and the Pacific Ocean.

Driving directions: From Highway 101 south of San Luis Obispo, take the Los Osos Valley Road exit, and head 12.1 miles west to the Montaña de Oro State Park entrance. Los Osos Valley Road becomes Pecho Valley Road en route. Continue 2.6 miles to the visitor center on the left and park.

Hiking directions: From the visitor center, walk east up the Islay Creek Campground road 0.4 miles to the Reservoir Flats Trail by campsite 40. Continue east on the footpath up the lush drainage, and traverse the hillside above the meandering Islay Creek. At 1.1 mile is a junction. The left fork is a short detour to the creek. Return and bear left, heading out of the shady canyon to an overlook. Descend from the ridge to Reservoir Flats, an open grassy bowl. Stay to the right at the signed Oats Peak Trail (Hike 30). Cross the sage-scrub hill and descend back to the visitor center.

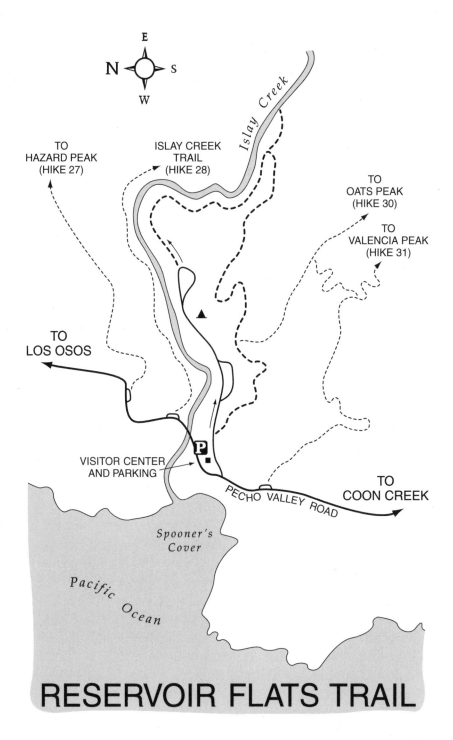

RESERVOIR FLATS TRAIL

Hike 30
Oats Peak Trail
Montaña de Oro State Park

Hiking distance: 5.5 miles round trip
Hiking time: 3 hours
Elevation gain: 1,300 feet
Maps: U.S.G.S. Morro Bay South
Montaña de Oro State Park map

Summary of hike: The Oats Peak Trail climbs from the ocean by Spooner's Cove to the second highest peak in the park at 1,373 feet. The trail crosses chaparral, thick brush and grassy meadows under the shadow of Valencia Peak. There are great views into the Coon Creek drainage and the folded interior canyons and ridges of the mountainous backcountry. To the north are views from Morro Bay to San Simeon .

Driving directions: From Highway 101 south of San Luis Obispo, take the Los Osos Valley Road exit, and head 12.1 miles west, to the Montaña de Oro State Park entrance. Los Osos Valley Road becomes Pecho Valley Road en route. Continue 2.6 miles to the visitor center on the left and park.

Hiking directions: Walk 50 yards east on the campground road, and take the signed Reservoir Flats Trail on the right by the maintenance buildings. Head uphill across the dry hillside to a signed trail split at 0.3 miles. The Reservoir Flats Trail (Hike 29) veers left. Go right on the Oats Peak Trail. At 0.6 miles is the first of two connector trails to Valencia Peak (Hike 31). Stay to the left, curving around to the east side of Valencia Peak to a saddle and signed junction. Bear left, following the ridge south to a second saddle near the summit of the 1,295-foot peak. Descend a short distance and begin the final half-mile ascent to Oats Peak. After enjoying the views, return along the same path.

To hike further, just beyond the peak is a junction. The Alan Peak Trail heads east for several miles to the peak. The Oats Peak Trail drops steeply into Coon Creek Canyon to the right.

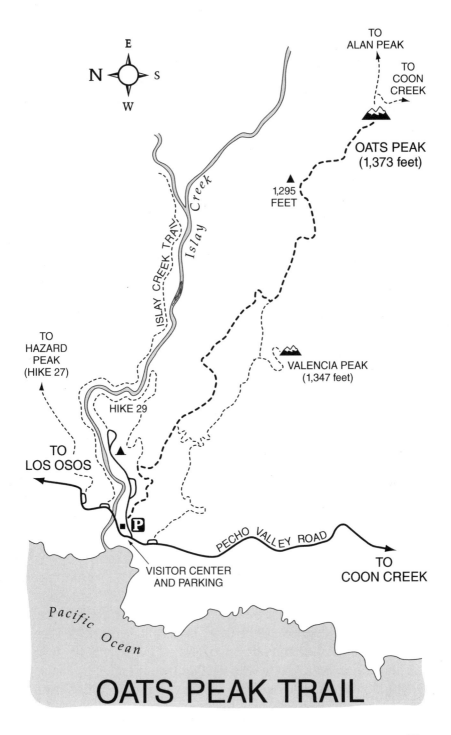

TO
ALAN PEAK

TO
COON
CREEK

OATS PEAK
(1,373 feet)

1,295
FEET

TO
COON
CREEK

ISLAY CREEK TRAIL

Islay Creek

TO
HAZARD
PEAK
(HIKE 27)

VALENCIA PEAK
(1,347 feet)

HIKE 29

TO
LOS OSOS

P

PECHO VALLEY ROAD

TO
COON CREEK

VISITOR CENTER
AND PARKING

Pacific
Ocean

OATS PEAK TRAIL

Hike 31
Valencia Peak Trail
Montaña de Oro State Park

Hiking distance: 4 miles round trip
Hiking time: 2 hours
Elevation gain: 1,150 feet
Maps: U.S.G.S. Morro Bay South
　　　　Montaña de Oro State Park map

Summary of hike: Valencia Peak, at 1,347 feet, has spectacular 360-degree views of Montaña de Oro, Morro Bay, Los Osos Valley and the rugged coastline from Point Sal to Piedras Blancas. The chain of morros leading to San Luis Obispo are in view. The trail crosses grasslands and straddles a ridge between two canyons before climbing directly up to the coastal peak.

Driving directions: From Highway 101 south of San Luis Obispo, take the Los Osos Valley Road exit, and head 12.1 miles west to the Montaña de Oro State Park entrance. Los Osos Valley Road becomes Pecho Valley Road en route. Continue 2.6 miles to the visitor center on the left. The trailhead parking area is on the left on Pecho Valley Road, a hundred yards past the visitor center.

Hiking directions: Hike east across the sage-covered flat on the signed trail. Head toward the base of the mountain, passing the Rattlesnake Flats Trail on the right. As the trail begins to climb, views of the scenic coastal plain open up. Switchbacks lead up to the first ridge above Spooner's Cove and the bluffs. Cross the grassy flat, in full view of Valencia Peak, to a junction at the base of the cone-shaped mountain. The left fork leads to the Oats Peak Trail (Hike 30). Take the right fork, climbing the edge of the mountain to a narrow ridge. Follow the ridge east up two steep sections with loose shale. At the base of the final ascent is another junction with the Oaks Peak Trail—stay to the right. Continue uphill, reaching the summit at two miles. After savoring the views, return along the same route.

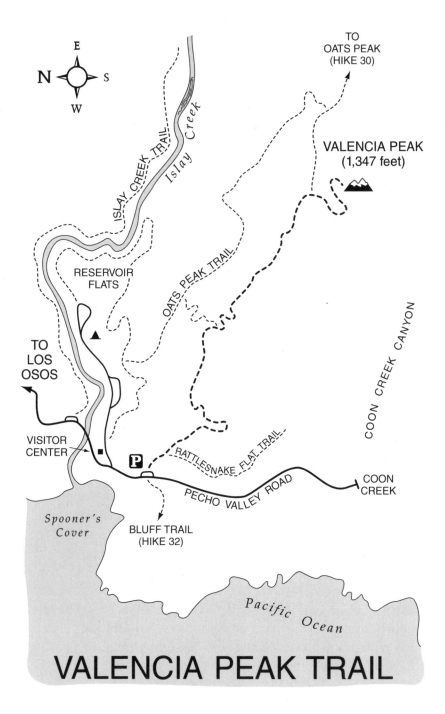

E
N ☀ S
W

TO
OATS PEAK
(HIKE 30)

Islay Creek

ISLAY CREEK TRAIL

VALENCIA PEAK
(1,347 feet)

RESERVOIR
FLATS

OATS PEAK TRAIL

COON CREEK CANYON

TO
LOS
OSOS

VISITOR
CENTER

P

RATTLESNAKE FLAT TRAIL

PECHO VALLEY ROAD

COON
CREEK

Spooner's
Cover

BLUFF TRAIL
(HIKE 32)

Pacific Ocean

VALENCIA PEAK TRAIL

Hike 32
Bluff Trail
Montaña de Oro State Park

Hiking distance: 3.4 miles round trip
Hiking time: 1.5 hours
Elevation gain: Level
Maps: U.S.G.S. Morro Bay South
       Montaña de Oro State Park map

Summary of hike: The Bluff Trail is an easy hike along one of the premier locations on the central California coastline. The trail snakes along the contours of a rugged network of eroding sandstone bluffs on a grassy marine terrace. Land extensions jut out into the ocean like fingers. There are hidden coves, sea caves, arches, sandy beaches, reefs, offshore outcroppings, clear tidepools, crashing surf, and basking seals and otters.

Driving directions: From Highway 101 south of San Luis Obispo, take the Los Osos Valley Road exit, and head 12.1 miles west to the Montaña de Oro State Park entrance. Los Osos Valley Road becomes Pecho Valley Road en route. Drive 2.6 miles to the visitor center on the left. The trailhead parking area is on the right on Pecho Valley Road, a hundred yards past the visitor center.

Hiking directions: Head west on the wide trail, and cross a wooden bridge to a trail fork. Take the right branch, following the cliff's edge along Spooner's Cove. Spur trails intersect the main trail throughout the hike, leading back to the road. The main path generally follows the cliff's edge, passing coves and rocky reefs. At Corallina Cove, the trail curves inland, crosses a footbridge over a narrow ravine, and returns to the ocean cliffs. Continue south past Quarry Cove, another sandy beach with tidepools. At 1.7 miles, is Grotto Rock, a prominent castle-shaped rock with caves near the PG&E fenceline. This is the turnaround spot. The trail leaves the coastline here and heads east to Pecho Valley Road. To return, retrace your steps.

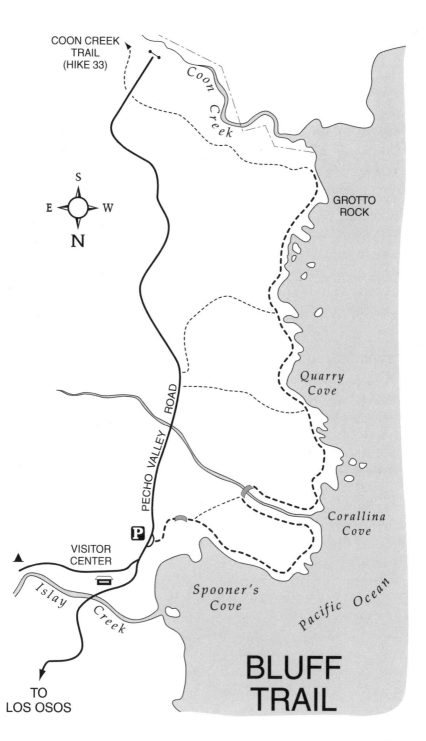

COON CREEK
TRAIL
(HIKE 33)

S
E · W
N

Coon Creek

GROTTO
ROCK

Quarry Cove

PECHO VALLEY ROAD

P

VISITOR
CENTER

Corallina Cove

Spooner's Cove

Pacific Ocean

Islay Creek

TO
LOS OSOS

BLUFF
TRAIL

Hike 33
Coon Creek Trail
Montaña de Oro State Park

Hiking distance: 5 miles round trip
Hiking time: 2.5 hours
Elevation gain: 200 feet
Maps: U.S.G.S. Morro Bay South and Port San Luis
Montaña de Oro State Park map

Summary of hike: The Coon Creek Trail heads up Coon Creek Canyon alongside the winding watercourse of the year-round stream. The trail crosses six bridges over the creek through the shade of the lush riparian corridor. Willows, maples, cottonwoods, oaks, cedars and cypress grow in the canyon with Spanish moss hanging from the branches.

Driving directions: From Highway 101 south of San Luis Obispo, take the Los Osos Valley Road exit, and head 12.1 miles west to the Montaña de Oro State Park entrance. Los Osos Valley Road becomes Pecho Valley Road en route. Continue 3.9 miles to the trailhead parking area on the left at the end of the road. It is 1.2 miles past the visitor center.

Hiking directions: Hike east past the trail sign and over a small ridge to a ravine. Bear right down wide steps, and follow the path along a fenceline to Coon Creek at 0.3 miles. Head up the canyon through the forest along the north side of the creek. Cross the first of six bridges over the creek past beautiful rock outcroppings. At 1.2 miles, the trail rises to an overlook of Coon Creek Canyon at a signed trail junction with the Rattlesnake Flats Trail on the left. Continue straight ahead up the shady canyon, and cross several more bridges. There is a junction on the left with the Oats Peak Trail at 2.4 miles. Continue a short distance ahead to the trail's end in a grove of old cedars and large oaks at an old cabin site. Return by retracing your steps.

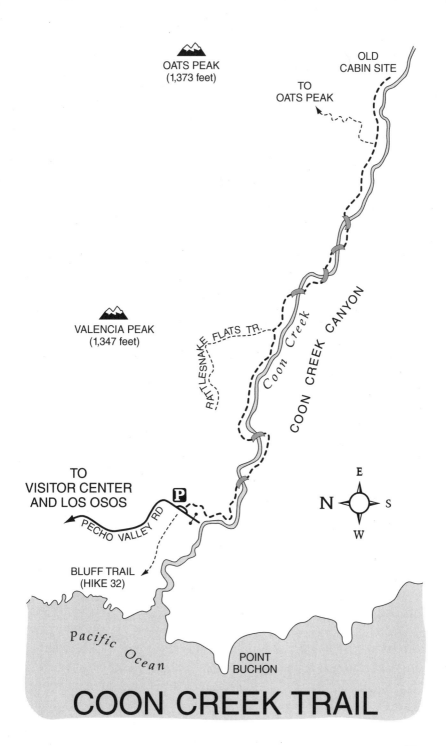

OATS PEAK
(1,373 feet)

OLD
CABIN SITE

TO
OATS PEAK

VALENCIA PEAK
(1,347 feet)

RATTLESNAKE FLATS TR.

Coon Creek

COON CREEK CANYON

TO
VISITOR CENTER
AND LOS OSOS

P

PECHO VALLEY RD

E
N · S
W

BLUFF TRAIL
(HIKE 32)

Pacific Ocean

POINT
BUCHON

COON CREEK TRAIL

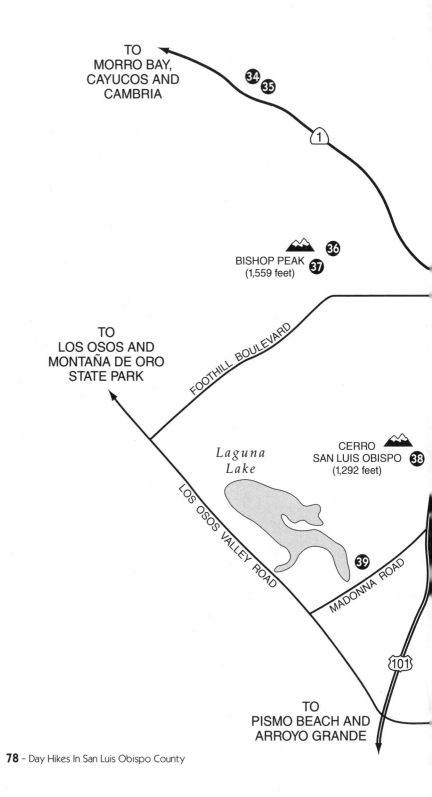

TO
MORRO BAY,
CAYUCOS AND
CAMBRIA

34 **35**

1

BISHOP PEAK **36**
(1,559 feet) **37**

TO
LOS OSOS AND
MONTAÑA DE ORO
STATE PARK

FOOTHILL BOULEVARD

*Laguna
Lake*

CERRO **38**
SAN LUIS OBISPO
(1,292 feet)

LOS OSOS VALLEY ROAD

39

MADONNA ROAD

101

TO
PISMO BEACH AND
ARROYO GRANDE

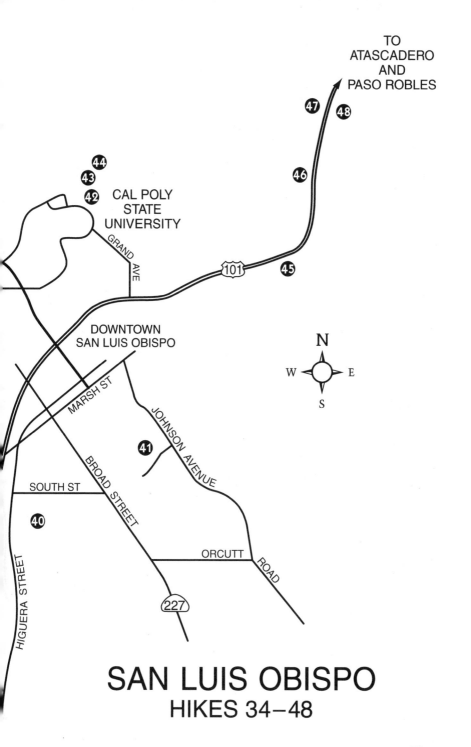

TO
ATASCADERO
AND
PASO ROBLES

47 **48**

44
43
42 CAL POLY
STATE
UNIVERSITY

46

GRAND AVE

101 **45**

N
W ← → E
S

DOWNTOWN
SAN LUIS OBISPO

MARSH ST

JOHNSON AVENUE

41

BROAD STREET

SOUTH ST

40

ORCUTT ROAD

HIGUERA STREET

227

SAN LUIS OBISPO
HIKES 34–48

Hike 34
Dairy Creek and El Chorro Loop
El Chorro County Regional Park

Hiking distance: 3 miles round trip
Hiking time: 1.5 hours
Elevation gain: 300 feet
Maps: U.S.G.S. San Luis Obispo

Summary of hike: El Chorro Regional Park encompasses more than 700 acres in El Chorro Valley at the base of the Santa Lucia Range. The park has shady oak and sycamore groves, hillside pastures, a botanical garden, campground, and miles of hiking and equestrian trails. This hike follows Dairy Creek, a year-round creek, up the valley and across the rolling hills to an overlook.

Driving directions: From Highway 101 in San Luis Obispo, take the Morro Bay/Highway 1 exit, and drive 5.5 miles northwest towards Morro Bay to El Chorro Regional Park on the right. It is located across the highway from Cuesta College. Turn right on the park road, and continue 0.8 miles to the Dairy Creek parking lot on the left by the locked gate.

Hiking directions: Hike up Dairy Creek Road past the locked trailhead gate. Follow the road through the rolling hillsides parallel to Dairy Creek to a junction at 0.8 miles. Bear left on the paved road, crossing the bridge over Dairy Creek. Pass a locked vehicle gate at one mile, and continue to an unpaved road on the left near the top of the hill. Take the path to the left, heading up the grassy hillside past several outcroppings to a trail split. You will return on the left trail, but for now take the right fork, reaching the top of the 664-foot hill at 1.6 miles. After enjoying the panoramic views, descend on the footpath to the left towards the water tank. A hundred yards before reaching the tank, bear left on the grassy road, heading east towards Dairy Creek Road. The trail curves left, completing the loop back at the trail split. Bear right, returning to the paved road. Retrace your steps back to the trailhead.

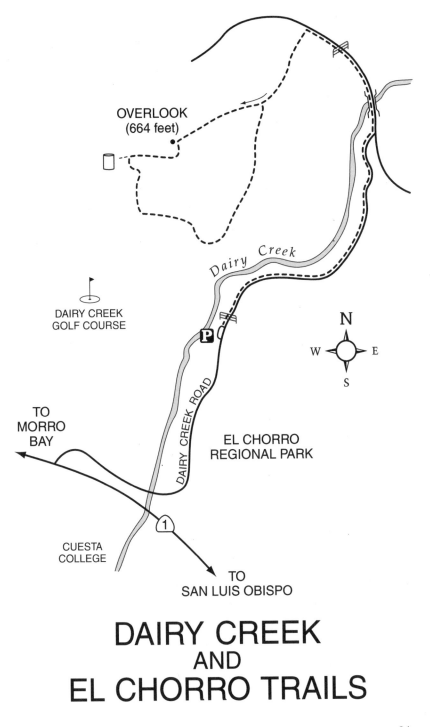

OVERLOOK
(664 feet)

Dairy Creek

DAIRY CREEK
GOLF COURSE

P

DAIRY CREEK ROAD

N
W   E
S

TO
MORRO
BAY

EL CHORRO
REGIONAL PARK

1

CUESTA
COLLEGE

TO
SAN LUIS OBISPO

DAIRY CREEK
AND
EL CHORRO TRAILS

Hike 35
Eagle Rock and Oak Woodlands Loop
El Chorro County Regional Park

Hiking distance: 2.5 mile loop
Hiking time: 1.5 hours
Elevation gain: 300 feet
Maps: U.S.G.S. San Luis Obispo

Summary of hike: The Eagle Rock Trail leads up the grassy hillside past Chumash mortar bowls to an overlook at a large rock outcropping. There are beautiful views of Chorro Valley, West Cuesta Ridge, Cuesta College, Dairy Creek Golf Course and the volcanic morros of Cerro Romualdo, Hollister Peak and Cerro Cabrillo.

Driving directions: Follow the driving directions for Hike 35 to the Dairy Creek parking lot.

Hiking directions: Hike up Dairy Creek Road past the trail-head gate for 0.1 mile to the signed nature trail on the right. Head to the right, leaving the paved road. The well-defined trail curves up the hillside through an oak forest. Beyond the forest, beautiful vistas open up of the surrounding area. At 0.4 miles the trail reaches a saddle at signpost 3. To the left of the trail is a rock slab with bowl-shaped holes. These holes were created by the Chumash Indians by grinding acorns into meal for bread. From the saddle, head east toward the prominent Eagle Rock to a signed junction. The left fork is the return route on the Oak Woodland Trail. Take the right fork and pass a wooden gate. Switchbacks lead up the grassy slope through scrub oak and chaparral to the overlook at Eagle Rock. Return 0.3 miles to the junction, and head north on the Oak Woodland Trail. The trail winds its way downhill through a forest of coast live oaks, reaching the Dairy Creek Road at 1.9 miles. Bear left, parallel to Dairy Creek, back to the trailhead.

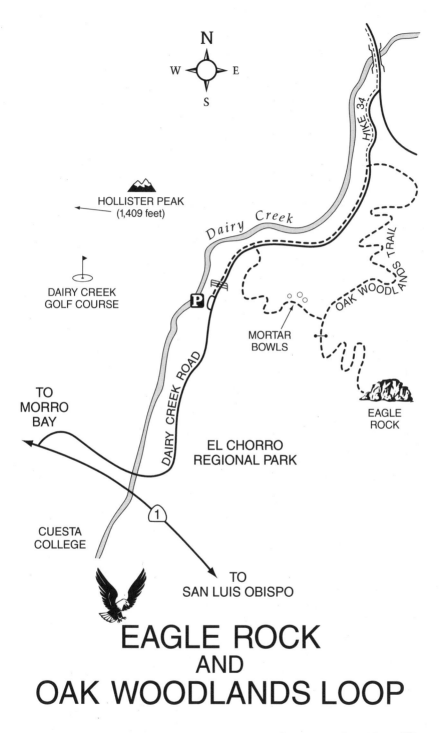

N
W E
S

HOLLISTER PEAK
(1,409 feet)

Dairy Creek

DAIRY CREEK
GOLF COURSE

P

HIKE 34

OAK WOODLANDS TRAIL

MORTAR
BOWLS

DAIRY CREEK ROAD

EAGLE
ROCK

TO
MORRO
BAY

EL CHORRO
REGIONAL PARK

1

CUESTA
COLLEGE

TO
SAN LUIS OBISPO

EAGLE ROCK
AND
OAK WOODLANDS LOOP

Hike 36
Felsman Loop

Hiking distance: 3.2 miles round trip
Hiking time: 1.5 hours
Elevation gain: 520 feet
Maps: U.S.G.S. San Luis Obispo

Summary of hike: The Felsman Loop, part of the Bishop Peak trail system, explores the forested northern foothills of Bishop Peak. The lower reaches of this reserve cross through open grasslands, shady woodland and chaparral. At the northern end of the open space, the trail follows a ridge overlooking the Santa Lucia Mountains, Poly Canyon, Cuesta Ridge, San Luis Obispo and the line of morros.

Driving directions: From downtown San Luis Obispo, head west on Foothill Boulevard to Patricia Drive and turn right. Continue 0.7 miles to the signed trailhead on the left. Park alongside the road.
From Los Osos Valley Road, take Foothill Boulevard 2.1 miles east to Patricia Drive, then follow the directions above.

Hiking directions: Head west past the trail sign on the wide path. At 150 yards, cross through the gate into a grove of coastal live oak. An asphalt road leads up to a water tank on the right. Bear left on the signed Bishop Peak Trail. Switchbacks lead uphill past an overlook of San Luis Obispo to a saddle and a junction. The left fork leads to the upper trailhead on Highland Drive. Bear right and zigzag up to a saddle at a fenceline, trail gate and junction. The left fork leads to Bishop Peak (Hike 37). Go right, joining an old ranch road. Head across the grassy hills and tree groves past two junctions. Follow the Felsman Loop along a ridge heading north to a signed footpath on the right. Bear right, traverse the hillside and cross the ravine. Switchbacks lead down to a trail gate. Continue around the contours of the hillside and around the left side of the water tank, completing the loop. Return to the trailhead on the left.

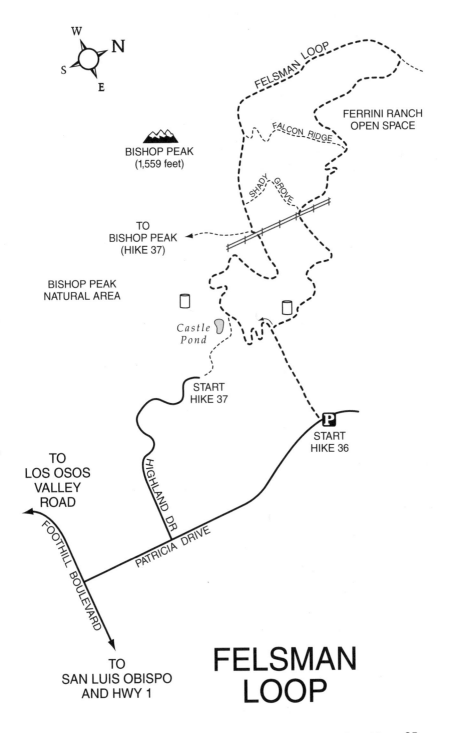

W N S E

FELSMAN LOOP

FERRINI RANCH
OPEN SPACE

FALCON RIDGE

BISHOP PEAK
(1,559 feet)

SHADY GROVE

TO
BISHOP PEAK
(HIKE 37)

BISHOP PEAK
NATURAL AREA

Castle
Pond

START
HIKE 37

START
HIKE 36

P

HIGHLAND DR.

TO
LOS OSOS
VALLEY
ROAD

FOOTHILL BOULEVARD

PATRICIA DRIVE

TO
SAN LUIS OBISPO
AND HWY 1

FELSMAN
LOOP

Hike 37
Bishop Peak Trail

Hiking distance: 4.5 miles round trip
Hiking time: 2 hours
Elevation gain: 950 feet
Maps: U.S.G.S. San Luis Obispo

Summary of hike: Bishop Peak, an ancient volcanic mountain, is the signature backdrop for the city of San Luis Obispo. The peak, which stands at 1,559 feet, has three distinctive peaks and is the highest in the chain of nine morros. The climb to the rocky peak winds through grasslands and oak woodlands. Near the summit, the trail becomes a scramble over massive granite boulders. From the peak is a panoramic 360-degree aerial view from the inland mountains to the coast. The views include San Luis Obispo, Los Osos Valley, El Chorro Valley and the entire chain of morros from Morro Rock to Islay Hill.

Driving directions: From downtown San Luis Obispo, head west on Foothill Boulevard to Patricia Drive and turn right. Continue 0.3 miles to Highland Drive and turn left. Drive 0.6 miles up to the signed trailhead at the end of the road.

From Los Osos Valley Road, take Foothill Boulevard 2.1 miles to Patricia Drive, then follow the directions above.

Hiking directions: Walk up the signed trail, following the fenceline into the shade of an oak forest. As you exit the forest, the trail merges with the path from the lower trailhead. Wind up the grassy hillside beneath the peak to a ridge. Follow the ridge west to a fenceline. Pass through the gate stile and bear left. (The right fork is the Felsman Loop, Hike 36). Head left through the woodland, passing a V-gate, and traverse the base of the mountain to the south. Switchbacks zigzag up the mountain while passing beautiful rock formations. The trail wraps around to the west side of Bishop Peak to the upper ridge. Weave up, over and around the boulders to the peak. Numerous paths reach the top. After marveling at the views, return along the same path.

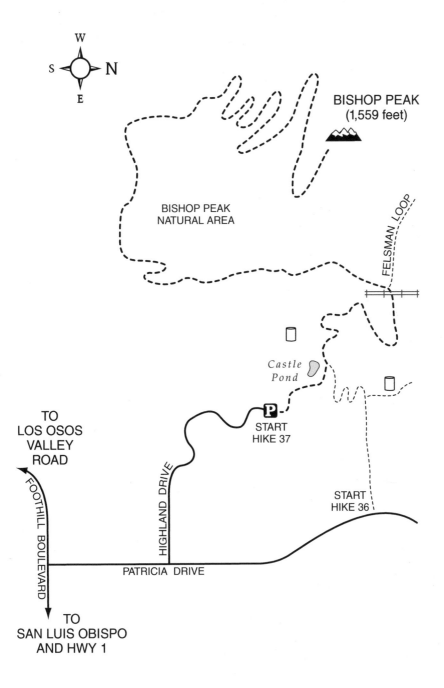

W **N**
S **E**

BISHOP PEAK
(1,559 feet)

BISHOP PEAK
NATURAL AREA

FELSMAN LOOP

Castle Pond

P
START
HIKE 37

TO
LOS OSOS
VALLEY
ROAD

START
HIKE 36

HIGHLAND DRIVE

FOOTHILL BOULEVARD

TO
SAN LUIS OBISPO
AND HWY 1

PATRICIA DRIVE

BISHOP PEAK TRAIL

Hike 38
Cerro San Luis Obispo
Maino Open Space

Hiking distance: 3 miles round trip
Hiking time: 1.5 hours
Elevation gain: 1,100 feet
Maps: U.S.G.S. San Luis Obispo

Summary of hike: Cerro San Luis Obispo is the large morro looming over San Luis Obispo with the big "M." It stands for Mission School, not Madonna or McDonald's. The trail up to this volcanic peak has great views of Laguna Lake (Hike 39) and Bishop Peak (Hike 37). From the summit there are views of San Luis Obispo, the Santa Lucia Mountains and the chain of morros to Morro Bay.

Driving directions: From downtown San Luis Obispo, take Higuera Street to the Highway 101 South on-ramp. Just before entering the freeway, turn right onto a dirt road and into the trailhead parking area on the right.

From Highway 101, exit on Marsh Street and cross the Marsh Street/Higuera Street intersection. Double back to Higuera by turning left on Carmel Street and again on Higuera Street. Then follow the directions above.

Hiking directions: Head north past the trailhead gate along the foothills. Curve left near large patches of prickly pear cactus. Long switchbacks lead up to the base of the mountain. Bear left at a trail split, cross a seasonal creek and go through a fence. Stay on the main trail past various side paths. As the trail curves up the western flank of the mountain, views open up of Laguna Lake and Bishop Peak. At the final approach to the summit, there is a trail fork. The trail loops around the knoll and returns to this spot. Take the left fork, hiking clockwise to a platform just below the final scramble to the rocky peak. After marveling at the views, return back to the main trail and continue circling the knoll. Return on the same path.

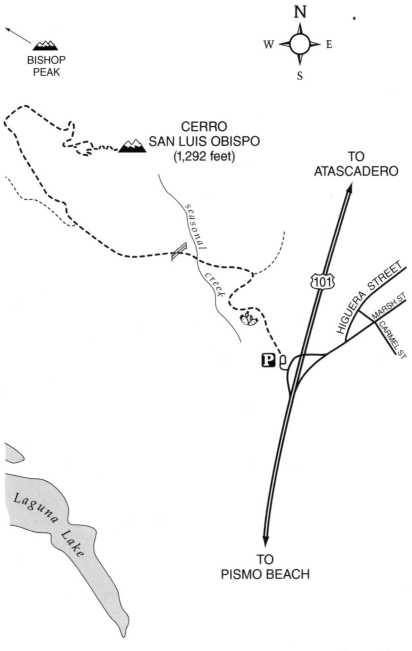

BISHOP
PEAK

N
W · E
S

CERRO
SAN LUIS OBISPO
(1,292 feet)

TO
ATASCADERO

seasonal creek

101

HIGUERA STREET

MARSH ST
CARMEL ST

P

TO
PISMO BEACH

Laguna Lake

CERRO SAN LUIS OBISPO

Hike 39
Laguna Lake Trail

Hiking distance: 1.5 miles round trip
Hiking time: 45 minutes
Elevation gain: Level
Maps: U.S.G.S. San Luis Obispo
　　　　 The Thomas Guide—San Luis Obispo County

Summary of hike: Laguna Lake Park encompasses 450 acres, including a 25-acre natural lake and a large undeveloped open space with hiking trails. The area was once used by the Chumash Indians for hunting and fishing. This level loop trail has great views of the surrounding hills, Laguna Lake and the line of Morros, including Cerro San Luis Obispo, Bishop Peak, Chumash Peak, Cerro Romualdo and Hollister Peak.

Driving directions: From Highway 101 in San Luis Obispo, exit on Madonna Road, and drive 0.4 miles southwest to Dalidio Drive. Turn right into Laguna Lake Park, and continue straight ahead 0.3 miles to the parking area on the left near the restrooms.

Hiking directions: Take the paved path northwest, crossing the wooden bridge to the signed entry gate. Follow the well-defined trail across the meadow parallel to the power poles. The volcanic peaks are prominent on the northern horizon. At 0.3 miles, take the unsigned trail to the right towards the base of the hillside. The trail heads north along the side of the hill to the park's northern boundary. Curve left and continue past a junction with the Meadow Trail to the fenceline. Cross through the gate and head left, returning to the south. At 1.2 miles, the trail reaches a grove of eucalyptus trees on the left and Laguna Lake on the right. Bear left through the grove of trees, completing the loop back at the trailhead gate.

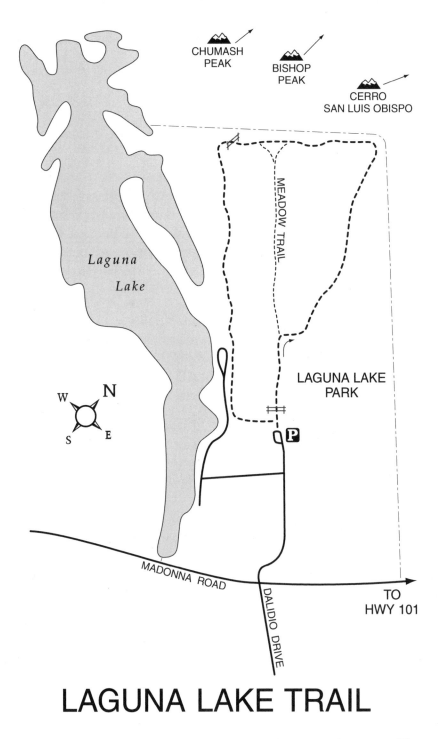

CHUMASH PEAK

BISHOP PEAK

CERRO SAN LUIS OBISPO

Laguna Lake

MEADOW TRAIL

LAGUNA LAKE PARK

N
W   E
S

P

MADONNA ROAD

DALIDIO DRIVE

TO HWY 101

LAGUNA LAKE TRAIL

Hike 40
South Hills Trail

Hiking distance: 2 miles round trip
Hiking time: 1 hour
Elevation gain: 400 feet
Maps: U.S.G.S. San Luis Obispo

Summary of hike: South Hills Open Space is a 60-acre gem in the city of San Luis Obispo. The one-mile gentle ascent to the rocky summit is highlighted by a birds-eye view of the city's folded green hills and surrounding valleys. The volcanic cones of Cerro San Luis Obispo and Bishop Peak are prominent landmarks to the north while the Santa Lucia Mountains border the city to the east and northeast.

Driving directions: From Higuera Street and South Street in San Luis Obispo, drive 0.3 miles east on South Street to Exposition Drive (by the Woodbridge sign). Turn right and continue 0.2 miles to the signed South Hills Open Space trailhead on the right, where Exposition Drive becomes Woodbridge Street. Park along the side of the road.

Hiking directions: Head southeast past the trail sign and towards the hills. Curve left, gaining elevation up the contours of the hillside. Pass through a gated fence. Continue up the hill past sculpted rock formations towards a saddle. Before reaching the saddle is a trail split. The right fork ends on the saddle by the open space boundary and an unpaved private road leading to a radio tower. Take the left fork, winding up the rocky hill to the summit. The trail follows the ridge southeast for a 360-degree panorama. Return the way you came.

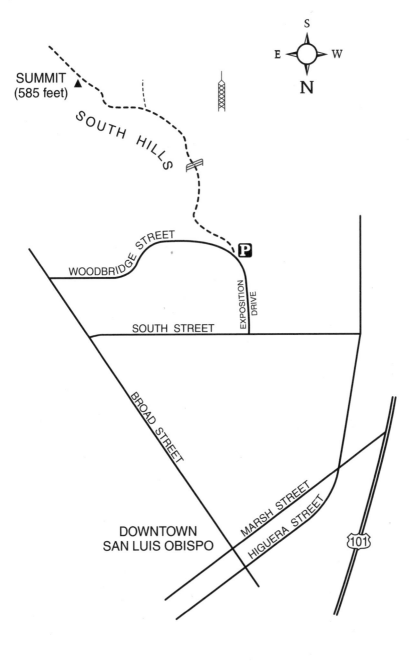

SOUTH HILLS TRAIL

Hike 41
Terrace Hill

Hiking distance: 0.8 miles round trip
Hiking time: 30 minutes
Elevation gain: 70 feet
Maps: U.S.G.S. San Luis Obispo

Summary of hike: The Terrace Hill Open Space is a pocket of nature inside the city of San Luis Obispo. The trail is a short, easy, scenic hike to an unobstructed terraced plateau. The morro-like rounded summit was bulldozed many years ago, creating a mesa. From the grassy flat are great panoramic views of the whole city. The Santa Lucia Range defines the city border to the north and east. Notice how the homes and development contour to the diverse geography around the city. Also within sight are Edna Valley and the chain of morros, including South Hills, Islay Hill, Orcott Knob, Cerro San Luis Obispo and Bishop Peak.

Driving directions: From Johnson Avenue in San Luis Obispo, take Bishop Street 0.1 mile southwest to the intersection with Augusta Court. Park on Augusta Court or Bishop Street east of Augusta. (Parking is not allowed on Bishop Street west of Augusta.) The signed Terrace Hill trailhead is on Bishop Street on the right, 50 yards west of Augusta Court.

Hiking directions: Walk southwest up Bishop Street to the signed and gated trailhead entrance on the right. Head northwest up the wide path to a large grassy flat. The path circles the perimeter of the terrace. A swinging bench is placed for viewing the volcanic cones of Cerro San Luis Obispo and Bishop Peak. A short, steep trail descends from the plateau to the north. The path levels out and circles the slope of the hill. As you round the hillside to the south, the trail returns to the entrance trail near the trailhead.

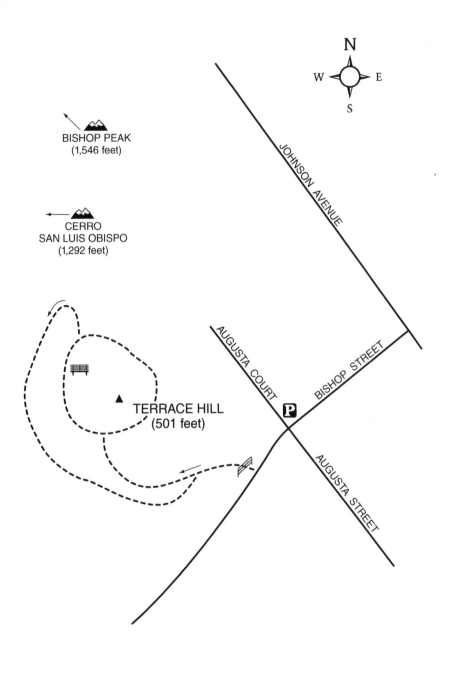

TERRACE HILL

Hike 42
Yucca Ridge Trail

Hiking distance: 3 miles round trip
Hiking time: 1.5 hours
Elevation gain: 700 feet
Maps: U.S.G.S. San Luis Obispo

Summary of hike: The Yucca Ridge Trail in Poly Canyon winds through an unmaintained botanical garden covered with yucca plants (the laughing plants of the desert). The trail ascends a ridge to the 1,139-foot Poly Canyon Overlook, above the Poly "P." From the top there are panoramic views of Poly Canyon, San Luis Obispo and the chain of morros.

Driving directions: From Highway 101 in San Luis Obispo, take the Grand Avenue/Cal Poly exit. Turn left onto Grand Avenue, and drive 0.7 miles to Perimeter Road in Cal Poly. Turn right and park 0.2 miles ahead in the H-4 parking lot on the right, just after crossing Poly Canyon Road. A parking permit is needed during the weekdays.

Hiking directions: Walk a short distance up Poly Canyon Road, and take the unpaved jogging road on the left. Continue up the canyon through a eucalyptus grove alongside Brizziolari Creek. At 0.9 miles is the university ranch and a beautiful rock arch. Twenty yards before reaching the arch is Baltimore Bridge a wooden footbridge crossing the creek on the right. Cross the bridge, taking the East Canyon Trail through a shady woodland. Near a wooden structure on the left, the trail curves right and climbs up the east canyon wall. Switchbacks and steps lead up to a signed junction with the Yucca Ridge Trail on the right. Go right, heading up the hillside on rock steps through a field of yuccas in an unmaintained botanical garden. The trail continues uphill to a saddle on the north flank of the mountain. Follow the path up the ridge to the 1,139-foot peak. From the peak are great 360-degree views. Return by retracing your steps.

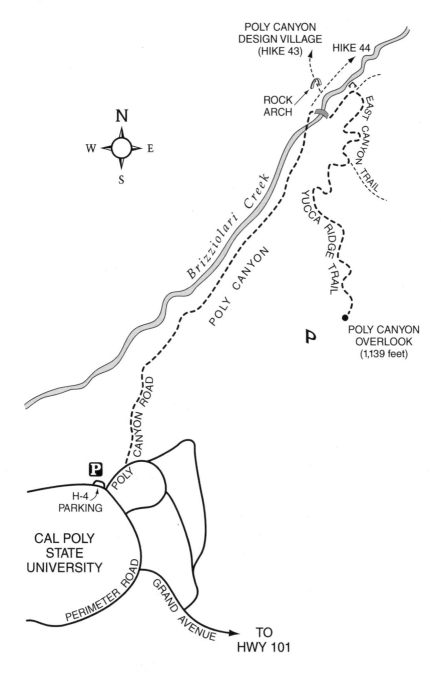

POLY CANYON
DESIGN VILLAGE
(HIKE 43)

HIKE 44

ROCK
ARCH

EAST CANYON TRAIL

N
W   E
S

Brizziolari Creek

POLY CANYON

POLY CANYON ROAD

YUCCA RIDGE TRAIL

P

POLY CANYON
OVERLOOK
(1,139 feet)

P

H-4
PARKING

CAL POLY
STATE
UNIVERSITY

PERIMETER ROAD

POLY

GRAND AVENUE

TO
HWY 101

YUCCA RIDGE TRAIL

Hike 43
Poly Canyon Design Village

Hiking distance: 3 miles round trip
Hiking time: 1.5 hours
Elevation gain: 300 feet
Maps: U.S.G.S. San Luis Obispo

Summary of hike: Poly Canyon Design Village is a collection of artistic, futuristic and sometimes humorous monuments from the architectural and engineering departments of Cal Poly. These monuments are works of art, attractively set among the rolling hills and grassy meadows in Poly Canyon. The experimental housing projects include a geodesic dome, an underground house, a shell house, a stick house, a greenhouse and a cantilevered platform in the shape of a ship bow. The trail to the village parallels Brizziolari Creek up the shady canyon.

Driving directions: From Highway 101 in San Luis Obispo, take the Grand Avenue/Cal Poly exit. Turn left onto Grand Avenue, and drive 0.7 miles to Perimeter Road in Cal Poly. Turn right and park 0.2 miles ahead in the H-4 parking lot on the right, just after crossing Poly Canyon Road. A parking permit is needed during the weekdays.

Hiking directions: Walk up Poly Canyon Road, bearing left on the jogging road. (See map on previous page.) Follow the unpaved canyon road northeast through the eucalyptus grove along the east side of Brizziolari Creek. At 0.9 miles is a junction with a beautiful stone arch on the left. Bear left under the arch and pass the trail map. Walk up the stone-lined path and cross the techtite bridge over the stream. Head up the draw past a picnic ground, large art sculptures and fascinating experimental structures. There are several looping routes across the rolling grassy meadows. Oak groves line the trickling streams through the village. The trails connect and return to the bridge and stone arch.

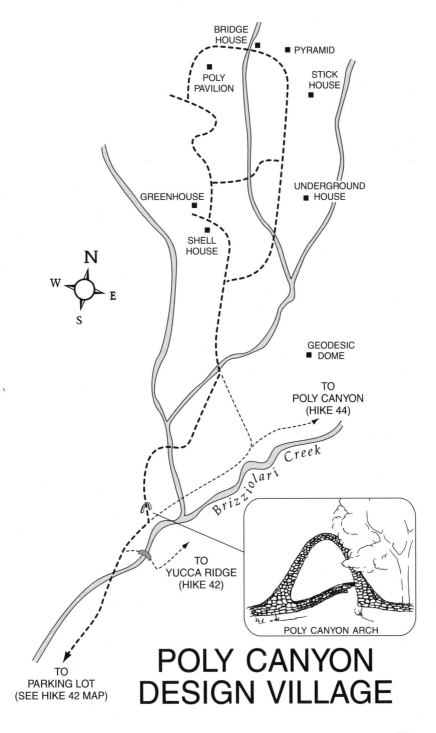

BRIDGE HOUSE

PYRAMID

POLY PAVILION

STICK HOUSE

N
W E
S

GREENHOUSE

UNDERGROUND HOUSE

SHELL HOUSE

GEODESIC DOME

TO POLY CANYON (HIKE 44)

Brizziolari Creek

TO YUCCA RIDGE (HIKE 42)

POLY CANYON ARCH

TO PARKING LOT (SEE HIKE 42 MAP)

POLY CANYON DESIGN VILLAGE

Hike 44
Poly Canyon

Hiking distance: 5.5 miles round trip
Hiking time: 2.5 hours
Elevation gain: 700 feet
Maps: U.S.G.S. San Luis Obispo
        The Mountain Biking Map for San Luis Obispo

Summary of hike: The Poly Canyon Trail follows a ranch road through the pastoral rolling hills alongside Brizziolari Creek behind the Cal Poly campus. The trail winds through the open space and rock outcroppings to the railroad tracks below Cuesta Ridge. The return route follows the north edge of the canyon through beautiful oak groves overlooking the canyon.

Driving directions: From Highway 101 in San Luis Obispo, take the Grand Avenue/Cal Poly exit. Turn left onto Grand Avenue, and drive 0.7 miles to Perimeter Road in Cal Poly. Turn right and park 0.2 miles ahead in the H-4 parking lot on the right, just after crossing Poly Canyon Road. A parking permit is needed during the weekdays.

Hiking directions: Walk a short distance up Poly Canyon Road, and take the unpaved jogging road on the left. Head up the canyon through the eucalyptus grove, parallel to Brizziolari Creek on the left. At 0.9 miles is a stone arch on the left and the university ranch straight ahead. Continue on the road, passing the ranch houses, barn and the first in a series of cattle gates. The trail heads up canyon parallel to Brizziolari Creek. Curve around the hillsides across the open rolling grasslands dotted with trees. Cross the creek to a corral at the base of the mountain. Bear left, parallel to a barbed wire fence as the grade steepens. Near the top of the hill, the trail curves left to a metal gate below the railroad tracks. Take the well-defined foot-path to the left, following the fenceline along the edge of the hillside. Cross through a beautiful oak grove and pass a barbed wire gate. Continue to an unsigned junction at a metal gate. Both routes return to the canyon floor. Straight ahead past the gate, the road gently curves down to the canyon. The footpath to the left descends rather steeply along the fenceline to the canyon. Bear right, returning to the trailhead.

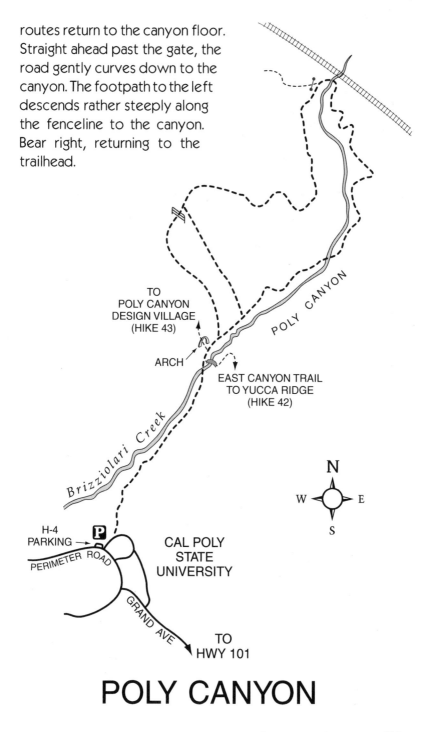

TO
POLY CANYON
DESIGN VILLAGE
(HIKE 43)

ARCH

POLY CANYON

EAST CANYON TRAIL
TO YUCCA RIDGE
(HIKE 42)

Brizziolari Creek

N
W   E
S

H-4
PARKING →
PERIMETER ROAD

CAL POLY
STATE
UNIVERSITY

GRAND AVE

TO
HWY 101

POLY CANYON

Hike 45
Reservoir Canyon Trail

Hiking distance: 2.8 miles round trip
Hiking time: 1.5 hours
Elevation gain: 200 feet
Maps: U.S.G.S. San Luis Obispo and Lopez Mountain

Summary of hike: The Reservoir Canyon Trail is found in an undeveloped open space maintained by the City of San Luis Obispo. It is a wonderful forested creekside trail that meanders up the canyon parallel to Reservoir Creek. Along the creek are cascades, small waterfalls and pools.

Driving directions: From Highway 101 in San Luis Obispo, drive 2 miles north and turn right on Reservoir Canyon Road. Drive 0.4 miles to the parking area on the left near the end of the road.

Hiking directions: Hike east up the road past the trailhead gate. The footpath leads up canyon through the foliage past several rock outcroppings. Cross Reservoir Creek two successive times in an oak woodland. At 0.5 miles, a side path branches right to a beautiful cascade with multiple small waterfalls and pools in a rock garden. After enjoying the pools, return to the main trail, and continue up canyon parallel to the creek. There is a trail split at 0.8 miles. The right fork descends to the creek by a steep embankment. Take the left fork 50 yards to a horse crossing on the right. Cross the creek, picking up the trail on the right by the embankment. Follow the trail southeast deeper into the canyon. At 1.2 miles, the trail crosses to the south side of the creek by a cascade, pool and remnants of an old bridge. Continue through the forest canopy to another creek crossing. After crossing, the trail fades near private property. Return along the same trail.

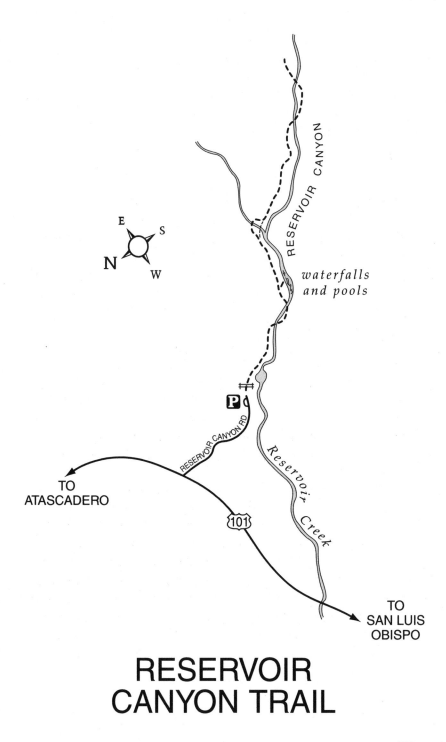

RESERVOIR
CANYON TRAIL

Hike 46
Stagecoach Road to Cuesta Pass

Hiking distance: 5.6 miles round trip
Hiking time: 2.5 hours
Elevation gain: 900 feet
Maps: U.S.G.S. Lopez Mountain and San Luis Obispo
Mountain Biking Map for San Luis Obispo

Summary of hike: The Stagecoach Road parallels Highway 101 and San Luis Obispo Creek through the shade of Cuesta Canyon while heading up to the Cuesta Grade summit. This historic road was formerly the Old Padre Trail, dating back to the 1700s. The Old Padre Trail was a primary route connecting San Luis Obispo with the northern inland valleys. Although the Stagecoach Road may be used by motor vehicles, it is primarily used for hiking and biking.

Driving directions: From Highway 101 in San Luis Obispo, drive 3.5 miles north to the Stagecoach Road turnoff on the left at the base of the Cuesta Grade. Turn left and park 0.2 miles ahead on the cement slab on the right.

Heading south on Highway 101, drive 3 miles down from the summit of the Cuesta Grade to Stagecoach Road on the right.

Hiking directions: Hike north on the unpaved road, and head up through the lush canyon under the shade of sycamore and oak trees. Cross a cattle guard and continue uphill. At 0.6 miles, the tree-lined road levels out, then begins the climb again at one mile. At 1.3 miles, the road curves sharply to the right as it begins to wind up the mountainside high above the canyon below. Cross a cascading stream at another sharp right bend as the road traverse the edge of the cliff. The road ends at Cuesta Pass in the parking area for the West Cuesta Ridge Road (Hike 47). To return, head back down the canyon.

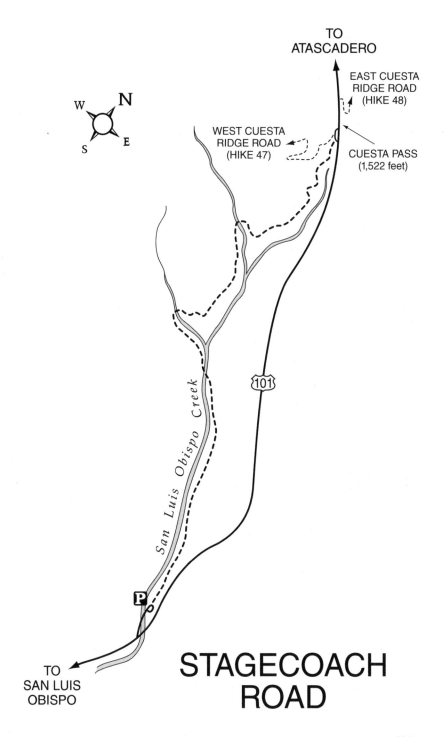

TO
ATASCADERO

EAST CUESTA
RIDGE ROAD
(HIKE 48)

WEST CUESTA
RIDGE ROAD
(HIKE 47)

CUESTA PASS
(1,522 feet)

101

San Luis Obispo Creek

P

TO
SAN LUIS
OBISPO

W N E S

STAGECOACH ROAD

Hike 47
West Cuesta Ridge Road
to Cuesta Ridge Botanical Area

Hiking distance: 7 miles round trip
Hiking time: 3 hours
Elevation gain: 850 feet
Maps: U.S.G.S. San Luis Obispo and Atascadero
Mountain Biking Map for San Luis Obispo

Summary of hike: The West Cuesta Ridge Road, also called the TV Tower Road, begins at the summit of the Cuesta Grade. The paved road winds up the terraced slopes of the mountain to some of the prime vistas in the county. It also passes through the 1,334-acre Cuesta Ridge Botanical Area in the Los Padres National Forest. The botanical garden has greenish serpentine bedrock and large groves of Sargent cypress, manzanita and pines. Throughout the hike are scenic overlooks. There are fantastic views of San Luis Obispo, Morro Bay, the Santa Lucia Wilderness, the Atascadero Hills, the Chorro and Los Osos Valleys, and the chain of morros. The rough, narrow road is open to motor vehicles but is primarily used as a hiking and biking route.

Driving directions: From Highway 101 in San Luis Obispo, drive 5 miles north to the Cuesta Grade summit. Continue one mile past the summit, and turn left at the first available turn. Return one mile, doubling back on Highway 101 to the truck parking area. Turn right and park by the trail information boards.

Hiking directions: To the left is the Stagecoach Road (Hike 46). Head up the paved road to the right, steadily winding uphill through groves of oaks. At 0.5 miles, views open up to the mountainous interior of the Los Padres National Forest. At one mile, bear right at a road fork, and continue along the contours of the mountain up to the ridge. Follow the ridge uphill to a road split below the radio tower at 2.6 miles. Bear left, curving around the hilltop to the signed Cuesta Ridge

Botanical Area at 3 miles. Follow the road through the botanical reserve, choosing your own turnaround spot. To hike further, the paved road ends at 5 miles by a Forest Service gate at the Cerro Alto trails (Hikes 14 and 15).

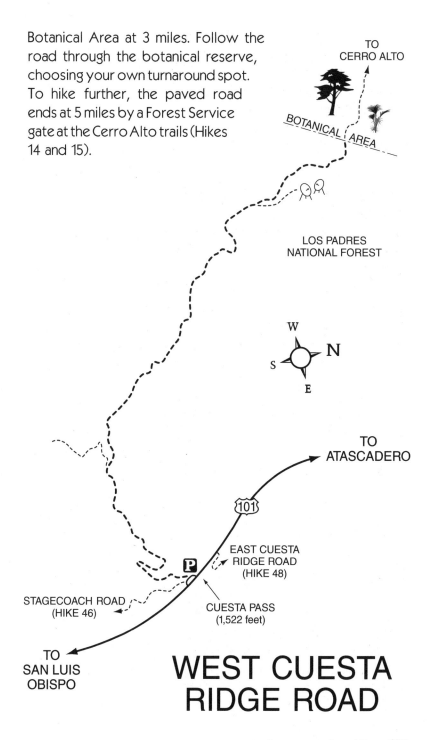

TO
CERRO ALTO

BOTANICAL AREA

LOS PADRES
NATIONAL FOREST

W
N
S
E

TO
ATASCADERO

101

EAST CUESTA
RIDGE ROAD
(HIKE 48)

P

STAGECOACH ROAD
(HIKE 46)

CUESTA PASS
(1,522 feet)

TO
SAN LUIS
OBISPO

WEST CUESTA RIDGE ROAD

Hike 48
East Cuesta Ridge Road

Hiking distance: 6 miles round trip
Hiking time: 3 hours
Elevation gain: 900 feet
Maps: U.S.G.S. San Luis Obispo and Lopez Mountain
        Mountain Biking Map for San Luis Obispo

Summary of hike: The East Cuesta Ridge Road, also called the Mount Lowe Road, begins at the summit of the Cuesta Grade. The unpaved road traverses the mountain along the Santa Lucia Wilderness through the shade of an oak, pine and manzanita forest. The hike offers a unique vantage point for fantastic views of San Luis Obispo and across the West Cuesta Ridge to the ocean, from Morro Bay to the Pismo Dunes. There are panoramic vistas of the Los Osos and Chorro Valleys, separated by the chain of volcanic morros. The road continues past the radio facility on Mount Lowe to Lopez Canyon at just under 5 miles.

Driving directions: From Highway 101 in San Luis Obispo, drive 5 miles north to the Cuesta Grade summit. Turn off the highway on the right in a parking pullout 150 yards beyond the "Cuesta Grade 1522 feet" sign. Drive 20 yards up the road to the right. Park in the pullout at the bend in the road.

Hiking directions: Hike up the road over the locked vehicle gate. Follow the road as it weaves up the grassy hillside dotted with oak trees. Continue uphill as the road traverses the mountainside, passing in and out of shady tree groves and crossing stream drainages. At 1.6 miles is a junction with a ranch road on the left. Continue on the main road, reaching the junction with the road to Mount Lowe at just under 3 miles. The road continues to a junction with the Lopez Canyon Trail at 3.7 miles and private property at 7 miles. Choose your own turnaround spot, and return along the same route.

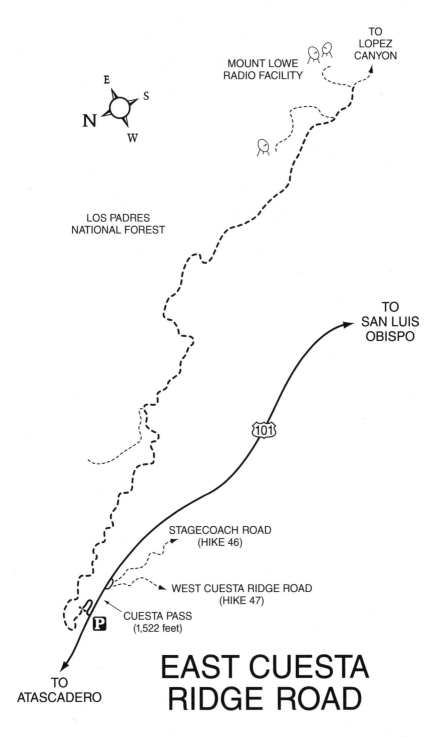

TO
LOPEZ
CANYON

MOUNT LOWE
RADIO FACILITY

N E S W

LOS PADRES
NATIONAL FOREST

TO
SAN LUIS
OBISPO

101

STAGECOACH ROAD
(HIKE 46)

WEST CUESTA RIDGE ROAD
(HIKE 47)

P

CUESTA PASS
(1,522 feet)

EAST CUESTA
RIDGE ROAD

TO
ATASCADERO

Hike 49
Grey Pine Trail to Eagle View
Santa Margarita Lake

Hiking distance: 3.2 miles round trip
Hiking time: 1.5 hours
Elevation gain: 230 feet
Maps: U.S.G.S. Santa Margarita Lake
       Santa Margarita Lake Regional Park map

map on next page

Summary of hike: The Grey Pine Trail weaves through the foothills at the base of the mountains next to Santa Margarita Lake. The hike winds through the shade of an oak-studded forest beneath magnificent sandstone rock outcroppings. The trail ends at Eagle View, a rocky point 326 feet above the lake. There are great views in every direction.

Driving directions: From San Luis Obispo, head 8 miles north on Highway 101, and take the Santa Margarita (Highway 58) exit. Drive east through Santa Margarita 3 miles, and bear right on Pozo Road, following signs to Santa Margarita Lake. Continue 6.4 miles to Santa Margarita Lake Road and turn left. Drive 1 mile to the entrance station. Take the road to the right 50 yards, and turn right into the Grey Pine Campground. The signed trail is on the left by the mobile home. A parking fee is required.

Hiking directions: Take the signed trail up the grassy slope, curving around the hillside beneath the imposing mountains and sandstone formations. Cross several ravines in the shade of the forest, gradually gaining elevation along the hillside. At 0.9 miles is a signed junction. The left fork leads to the lake, returning to Grey Pine Campground on the park road. Take the right fork towards White Oak Flat. The footpath leads to a trail split on a ridge overlooking the flat. Bear left up the ridge to another signed trail split. Take the left fork uphill towards Eagle View. Hike along the ridge past two overlooks with benches. The last 0.2 miles follows a rocky narrow path, ending at a steep point high above the lake. Return by retracing your steps.

Hike 50
Lone Pine Trail to Vaca Flat
Santa Margarita Lake

Hiking distance: 2.6 miles round trip
Hiking time: 1.5 hours
Elevation gain: 500 feet
Maps: U.S.G.S. Santa Margarita Lake
Santa Margarita Lake Regional Park map

map on next page

Summary of hike: Vaca Flat is a beautiful waterfront picnic area surrounded by mountains on a peninsula jutting into Santa Margarita Lake. The Lone Pine Trail winds through an oak forest past sculpted sandstone formations and magnificent overlooks en route to Vaca Flat.

Driving directions: Follow the driving directions for Hike 49 to the Santa Margarita Lake entrance station. At the entrance station, take the road to the right 1 mile to the signed Lone Pine trailhead on the right. Park in the White Oak Flat lot on the left, just past the trail. A parking fee is required.

Hiking directions: Cross the park road and head east past the trail sign to a junction 100 yards ahead. To the right, is the Grey Pine Trail (Hike 49). Take the left fork across the grassy hillside with views of beautiful sandstone formations. Switchbacks lead sharply up the hillside through oak groves to a bench at an overlook of Santa Margarita Lake. After resting, continue uphill past massive sandstone outcroppings and great views. Shortly beyond the formation is an unsigned junction at 0.6 miles. The right fork leads 60 yards uphill to another bench and overlook. Follow the left fork, curving through the mountainous terrain. The trail descends past more outcroppings to the unpaved road to Vaca Flat Picnic Area. Pick up the signed trail across the road, and continue along the contours of the hillside to the north-facing slope above the lake. Descend to the east to Vaca Flat, a grassy picnic area on the banks of the lake. Return by retracing your steps.

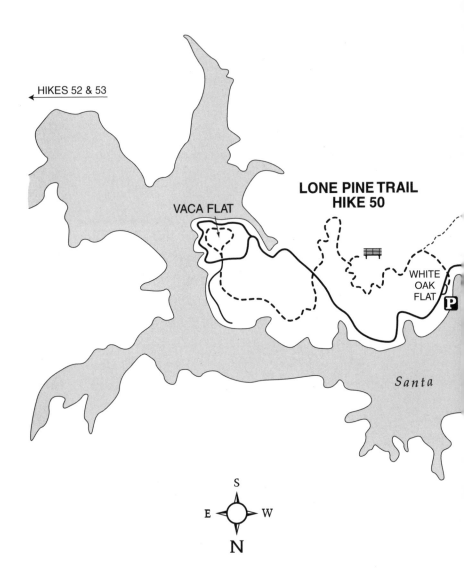

← HIKES 52 & 53

LONE PINE TRAIL
HIKE 50

VACA FLAT

WHITE
OAK
FLAT

Santa

S
E ✦ W
N

SANTA MARGARITA LAKE
HIKES 49 and 50

GREY PINE TRAIL
HIKE 49

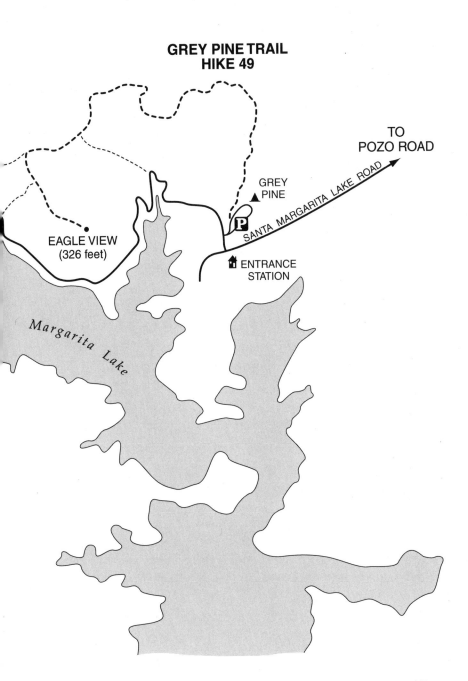

TO
POZO ROAD

GREY
PINE

SANTA MARGARITA LAKE ROAD

P

EAGLE VIEW
(326 feet)

ENTRANCE
STATION

Margarita Lake

Hike 51
Rinconada Trail

Hiking distance: 4 miles round trip
Hiking time: 2 hours
Elevation gain: 600 feet
Maps: U.S.G.S. Santa Margarita Lake
Mountain Biking Map for Eastern SLO County

Summary of hike: The Rinconada Trail is a beautiful back-country hike in the Los Padres National Forest. Switchbacks lead up the grassy slopes to a ridge with scenic vista points of the Santa Lucia Mountains, Lopez Canyon, Santa Margarita Valley and Pozo Valley.

Driving directions: From San Luis Obispo, head 8 miles north on Highway 101, and take the Santa Margarita (Highway 58) exit. Drive east through Santa Margarita 3 miles, and bear right on Pozo Road, following signs to Santa Margarita Lake. Continue 9.2 miles to the signed trail on the right. Turn right and drive 0.1 mile to the end of the road at the trailhead parking lot. A parking fee is required.

Hiking directions: Hike past the trail sign on the well-defined path. Head through stands of oak trees, winding up the grassy slopes. The remains of Rinconada Mine can be seen to the right. Switchbacks lead up to the ridge with great views of the mountains and valleys. At 1.5 miles, cross a fenceline and metal gate to a flat, grassy saddle. Bear to the right past a cairn (manmade rock mound), and descend across the grassy slopes on a rocky path into the next drainage south. At two miles, a short spur trail drops down to the left, joining the unpaved Hi Mountain Road. Take the road a hundred yards to the right to the signed Little Falls Trail on the left. This is the turnaround spot. Return by retracing your steps.

To hike further, the trail descends steeply into Lopez Canyon to Little Falls (Hike 67).

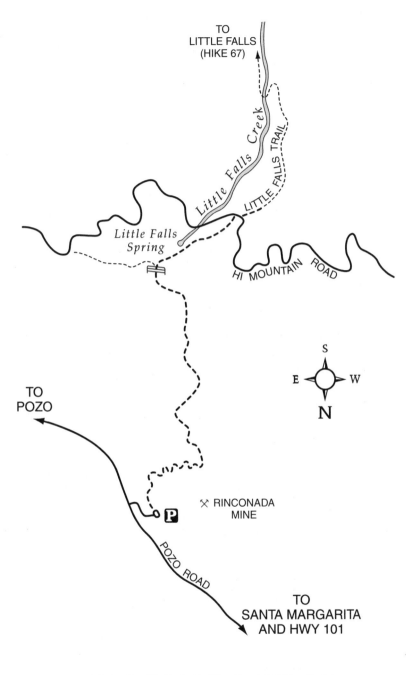

TO
LITTLE FALLS
(HIKE 67)

Little Falls Creek

LITTLE FALLS TRAIL

Little Falls
Spring

HI MOUNTAIN ROAD

S

E ✦ W

N

TO
POZO

× RINCONADA
MINE

P

POZO ROAD

TO
SANTA MARGARITA
AND HWY 101

RINCONADA TRAIL

Hike 52
Sandstone Trail
Santa Margarita Lake

Hiking distance: 5 miles round trip
Hiking time: 2.5 hours
Elevation gain: 200 feet
Maps: U.S.G.S. Santa Margarita Lake
Santa Margarita Lake Regional Park map

Summary of hike: The Sandstone Trail begins at the eastern access to Santa Margarita Lake. The trail traverses the hillside through oak groves on the south side of the lake. The hike leads to scenic overlooks of the surrounding mountains and to a seasonal 40-foot waterfall. The stream cascades over a beautiful sandstone rock formation.

Driving directions: From San Luis Obispo, head 8 miles north on Highway 101, and take the Santa Margarita (Highway 58) exit. Drive east through Santa Margarita 3 miles, and bear right on Pozo Road, following signs to Santa Margarita Lake. Continue 14 miles to River Road and turn left. Drive 1.7 miles to the East River Trail access on the left. Park in the lot at the trailhead. A parking fee is required.

Hiking directions: Walk northwest past the trail gate on the East River Access Road. The first half mile crosses the rolling foothills dotted with oak trees to a signed junction. The right fork is the Blinn Ranch Trail (Hike 53). Take the Sandstone Trail to the left, and wade across the slow rolling Salinas River. After crossing, head west on the level, well-defined trail. At one mile, the trail enters the forested canyon and winds up the hillside to the ridge. Follow the ridge past several overlooks of Santa Margarita Lake. Descend into McNeil Canyon, curving south to a seasonal waterfall at an inlet stream to the lake. Continue to the second lake finger at an outlet stream by the remnants of a cement bridge. This is a good turnaround spot.
To hike further, the old ranch road parallels the stream south.

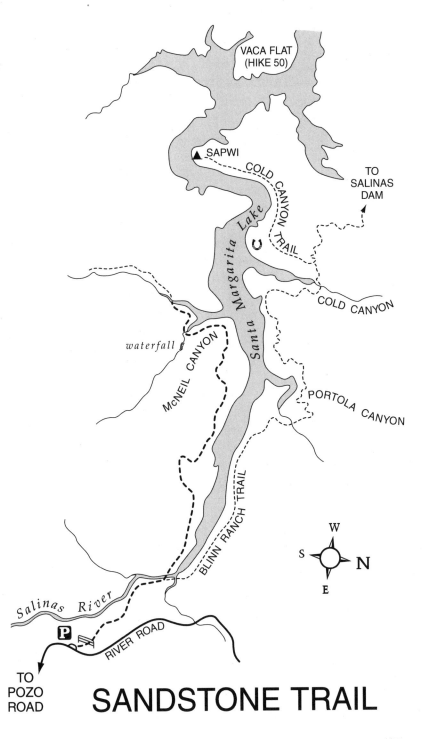

VACA FLAT
(HIKE 50)

▲ SAPWI

COLD CANYON TRAIL

TO
SALINAS
DAM

Santa Margarita Lake

COLD CANYON

waterfall

McNEIL CANYON

PORTOLA CANYON

BLINN RANCH TRAIL

Salinas River

P

RIVER ROAD

TO
POZO
ROAD

W
S ✳ N
E

SANDSTONE TRAIL

Hike 53
Blinn Ranch Trail
Santa Margarita Lake

Hiking distance: 6 miles round trip
Hiking time: 3 hours
Elevation gain: 250 feet
Maps: U.S.G.S. Santa Margarita Lake
Santa Margarita Lake Regional Park map

Summary of hike: The Blinn Ranch Trail is an old ranch road that follows the north edge of Santa Margarita Lake from the eastern end of the lake. The hike begins along the pastoral rolling grasslands dotted with pines and oaks. The trail winds through Portola Canyon and Cold Canyon, with several stream crossings and scenic overlooks of the lake.

Driving directions: Follow the driving directions for Hike 52 to the trailhead.

Hiking directions: Walk through the trailhead gate and head west on the East River Road Access. The road curves through the pastureland with groves of oaks and pines. At 0.5 miles is a signed trail split. The Sandstone Trail (Hike 52) bears to the left. Take the right fork on the Blinn Ranch Trail past sandstone outcroppings. Cross planks over the inlet stream and follow the creek downstream. At 1.5 miles, curve up the hillside to views of the east arm of the lake. Descend and cross another inlet stream in Portola Canyon. Wind through the canyon past numerous sandstone outcroppings. At 2.4 miles, the trail snakes through an oak grove with great views above the lake. Curve around the west side of Cold Canyon, crossing a third inlet stream below the sandstone cliffs. Ascend the hill to a signed junction with the Cold Canyon Trail. This is the turnaround spot.

To hike further, the 8-mile long Blinn Ranch Trail continues to the west end of the lake by Salinas Dam. The Cold Canyon Trail (named Sapwi Trail on various maps) descends a half mile to the horse camp and 1.35 miles to Sapwi Camp.

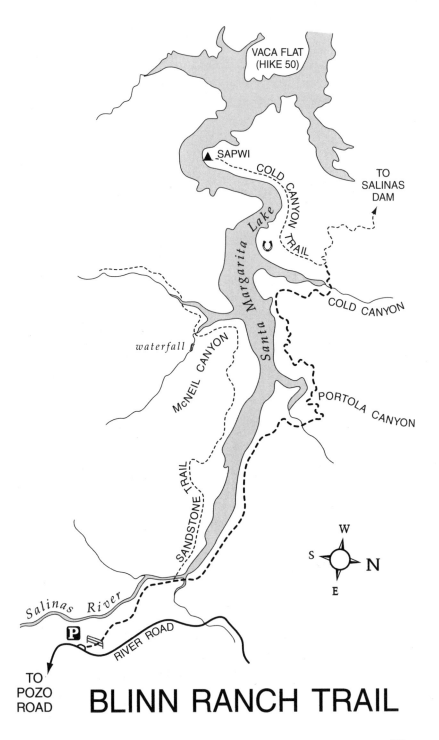

VACA FLAT
(HIKE 50)

SAPWI

COLD CANYON TRAIL

TO
SALINAS
DAM

C

COLD CANYON

Santa Margarita Lake

waterfall

McNEIL CANYON

PORTOLA CANYON

SANDSTONE TRAIL

Salinas River

W

S ✦ N

E

P

RIVER ROAD

TO
POZO
ROAD

BLINN RANCH TRAIL

Hike 54
Pecho Coast Trail

Free docent-led hike on PG&E land
Reservations required: (805) 541-8735

Hiking distance: 3.5—7.4 miles round trip
Hiking time: 4 hours—7 hours
Elevation gain: 440 feet
Maps: U.S.G.S. Port San Luis

Summary of hike: The Pecho Coast Trail curves around the northern point of San Luis Obispo Bay from Port San Luis towards Moñtana de Oro State Park. There are two docent-led hikes across the privately owned PG&E land. Both hikes follow the steep cliffs to Point San Luis and the Port San Luis Lighthouse, a two-story Victorian redwood structure built in 1890. It is a great spot for watching the annual migration of the gray whales. The longer hike continues across the coastal bluffs and pastureland to an oak grove in Rattlesnake Canyon.

Driving directions: From Highway 101 in Pismo Beach, take the Avila Beach Drive exit. Head 4.2 miles west, passing the town of Avila, to the PG&E Diablo Canyon Power Plant entrance on the right at Port San Luis Harbor. Park in the wide area on the left, across the road from the PG&E entrance gate.

Hiking directions: Naturalists will lead the hike, providing geological, botanical and historical details. Begin by walking up the steps past a locked gate west of the PG&E station. Ascend the hillside overlooking the bay and three piers. Bear left on the lighthouse road to the Pecho Coast Trail; take the footpath left. Descend the hillside towards the ocean. Follow the contour of the mountains on a cliffside trail 200 feet above the ocean. The trail passes Smith Island and Whaler's Island. Continue around the point, rejoining the paved road to the lighthouse.
    The longer hike continues past the lighthouse, crossing the coastal terrace and grasslands to an oak woodland in Rattlesnake Canyon for lunch. Return by retracing your steps.

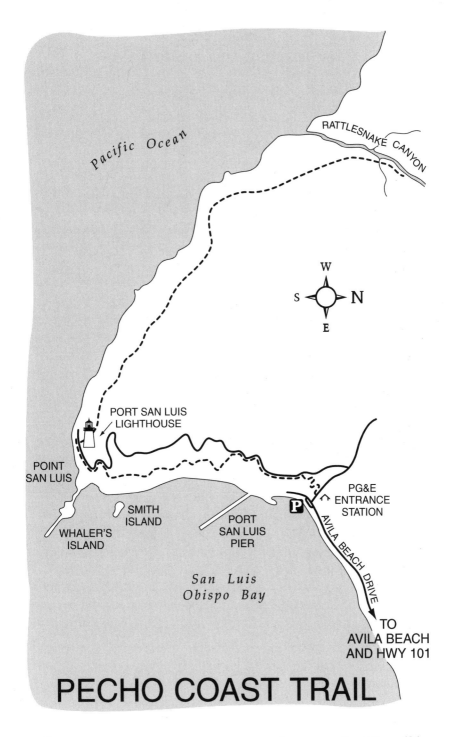

Pacific Ocean

RATTLESNAKE CANYON

W
S ◆ N
E

PORT SAN LUIS
LIGHTHOUSE

POINT
SAN LUIS

SMITH
ISLAND

PORT
SAN LUIS
PIER

WHALER'S
ISLAND

PG&E
ENTRANCE
STATION

P

AVILA BEACH DRIVE

San Luis
Obispo Bay

TO
AVILA BEACH
AND HWY 101

PECHO COAST TRAIL

Hike 55
Cave Landing and Pirate's Cove

Hiking distance: 2 miles round trip
Hiking time: 1 hour
Elevation gain: 120 feet
Maps: U.S.G.S. Pismo Beach
　　　　The Thomas Guide—San Luis Obispo County

Summary of hike: Cave Landing, also known as Mallagh Landing, is a spectacular rocky promontory that juts out 150 feet into the bay, forming a natural pier. This beautiful formation has caves and coves, including an arch carved through the cliffs near the headland point. From the point are great views of the steep, chiseled cliffs along the rugged coastline. Pirate's Cove, a crescent-shaped, clothing-optional beach, sits at the base of the hundred-foot cliffs.

Driving directions: From Highway 101 in Pismo Beach, exit on Avila Beach Drive. Head 2 miles west to Cave Landing Road and turn left. Continue 0.5 miles to the trailhead parking lot on the right at the end of the road.

Hiking directions: The trail heads southeast towards the rocky point overlooking the Shell Beach and Pismo Beach coastline. At 20 yards is a junction. Bear left to a trail split 0.2 miles ahead. The left fork descends to Pirate's Cove. Before descending, take the right fork to another trail split. To the right is a natural arch cave leading to an overlook. To the left is another overlook at the edge of the cliffs. Return to the junction and bear right, curving gently down the cliffs to Pirate's Cove. Continue along the sandy beach beneath the cliffs. Return along the same path.

For an additional 0.6-mile hike, take the wide path heading west at the opposite end of the trailhead parking area. The trail leads down to a flat, grassy plateau. From the plateau, a path follows the cliff's edge to the left. Caves can be seen along the base of the cliffs. Return the way you came.

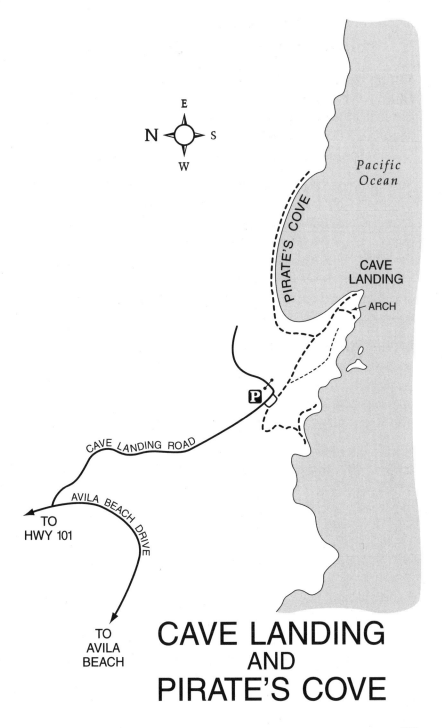

Pacific
Ocean

PIRATE'S COVE

CAVE
LANDING

ARCH

P

CAVE LANDING ROAD

AVILA BEACH DRIVE

TO
HWY 101

TO
AVILA
BEACH

CAVE LANDING
AND
PIRATE'S COVE

Hike 56
Bob Jones City to the Sea Bike Trail

Hiking distance: 5.6 miles round trip
Hiking time: 2.5 hour
Elevation gain: 150 feet
Maps: U.S.G.S. Pismo Beach
        The Thomas Guide—San Luis Obispo County

Summary of hike: The Bob Jones City to the Sea Bike Trail (originally known as the Avila Valley Bike Trail) follows the old Pacific Coast Railroad right-of-way. It is used as a hiking, jogging and biking route. The paved trail winds through the forested valley alongside San Luis Obispo Creek towards Avila Beach. From the trail are views of bridges spanning the wide creek (photo on back cover), the Avila Beach Golf Course, the town of Avila and the Pacific Ocean.

Driving directions: From Highway 101 in Pismo Beach, exit on Avila Beach Drive. Head west 0.3 miles to Ontario Road at Avila Hot Springs Spa. Turn right and continue 0.3 miles, crossing the bridge over San Luis Obispo Creek, to the trailhead parking lot on the right.

Hiking directions: Cross Ontario Road and pick up the signed trail heading west. The trail immediately enters a lush forest parallel to San Luis Obispo Creek. Although you are near the creek, the dense foliage makes access to the creek nearly impossible. At 0.7 miles, cross a bridge over See Canyon Creek, and then cross San Luis Bay Drive at one mile. Continue past Avila Bay Club on the right and the creek on the left to the trail's end at Blue Heron Drive. Bear left on the private road, staying close to the creek. The road curves around the hillside overlooking the creek, bridges and golf course. At the first bridge spanning the creek is a junction. The left fork heads across the bridge to Avila Beach Drive. The right fork continues to the golf course entrance by Mulligans Restaurant. Both paths lead to Avila Beach. To return, take the same trail back.

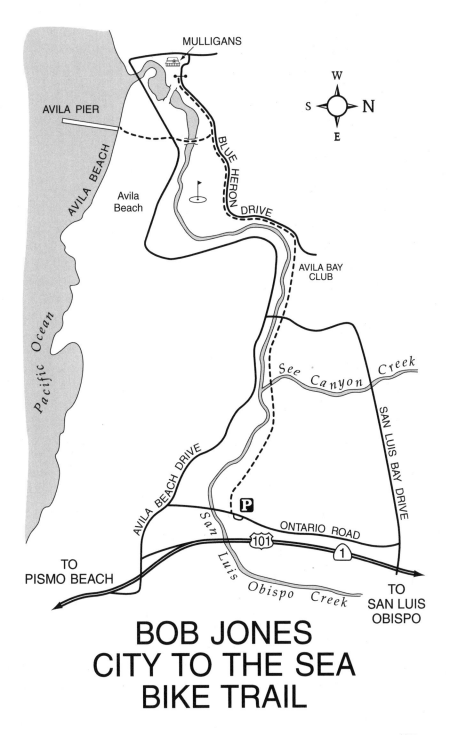

BOB JONES
CITY TO THE SEA
BIKE TRAIL

Hike 57
The Shell Beach Bluffs Walking Path

Hiking distance: 2 miles round trip
Hiking time: 1 hour
Elevation gain: 70 feet
Maps: U.S.G.S. Pismo Beach
      The Thomas Guide—San Luis Obispo County

Summary of hike: The Shell Beach Bluffs Walking Path parallels the scalloped coastal cliffs 100 feet above Pirate's Cove, a clothing-optional white sand beach. From the trail are views of Cave Landing, a promontory with a natural arch cave carved through the rocky cliffs (Hike 55). Sea otters and sea lions are frequently seen near the ocean rocks.

Driving directions: From Highway 101 in Pismo Beach, exit on Avila Beach Drive. Head west to the first street—Shell Beach Drive—and turn left. Continue 0.3 miles to El Portal Drive and turn right. Drive 0.6 miles, bearing right on Indio Drive, to the trailhead parking lot at the end of the road.

Hiking directions: Hike west on the paved walkway above the rugged coastline along the cliffs overlooking the ocean. The trail joins Bluffs Drive for 100 yards, a private road which passes a few luxury homes. At a trail fork, the left trail is a short detour that leads 30 yards to an overlook. Continue on the right fork to the end of the path. Follow the gated, unpaved road uphill, curving around the west side of the cove. The trail ends at the parking lot by Cave Landing, the trailhead to the promontory and Pirate's Cove (Hike 55). Return by retracing your steps.

To add one mile to your hike, from the trailhead parking lot, walk back up Indio Drive to the round-about. A well-defined trail—an abandoned, unpaved road—heads east along the base of the hillside parallel to El Portal Drive. The trail ends at Shell Beach Road at the north edge of the Sunset Palisades subdivision.

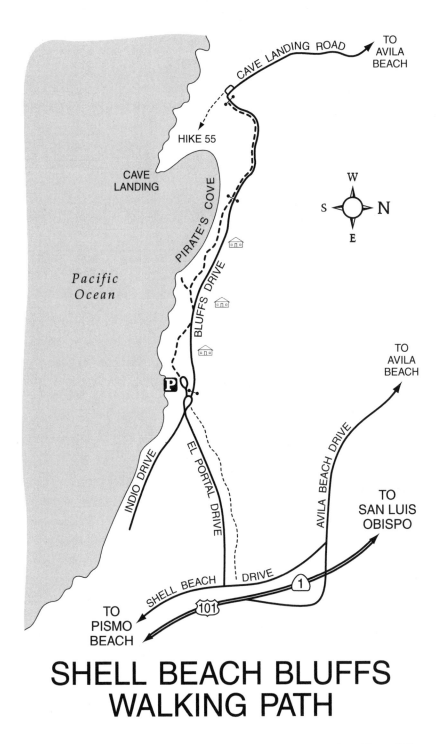

SHELL BEACH BLUFFS
WALKING PATH

Hike 58
Chumash Park

Hiking distance: 1 mile round trip
Hiking time: 30 minutes
Elevation gain: 50 feet
Maps: U.S.G.S. Arroyo Grande NE
       The Thomas Guide—San Luis Obispo County

Summary of hike: Chumash Park in Pismo Beach is in a small forested canyon with majestic old oaks. Homes are built on the hillside ridges overlooking the canyon. The north-facing hillside is covered in oak trees. A seasonal stream flows through the lush drainage. The trail winds up the draw on an unpaved ranch access road. Plans are in progress for a trail and bridge crossings through the oaks on the south side of the canyon.

Driving directions: Heading southbound on Highway 101 in Pismo Beach, take the 4th Street exit and turn left to 4th Street. Head 0.1 mile east to James Way. Heading northbound on Highway 101, take the 4th Street/Five Cities Drive exit to 4th Street. Turn right one block to James Way. Turn left on James Way and drive 0.1 mile to Ventana Drive. Turn right and make a quick right again by the Chumash Park sign. Park alongside the curb. For a secondary parking area, drive 0.2 miles on Ventana Drive. Turn left and park on La Garza.

Hiking directions: Walk east to the end of the paved road and past the metal gate. Continue on the dirt access road up the forested draw. A gentle rise leads to views of grazing cows and rolling pastureland. Cross over the seasonal stream to the end of the trail at the fenced ranch boundary. Return by retracing your steps.

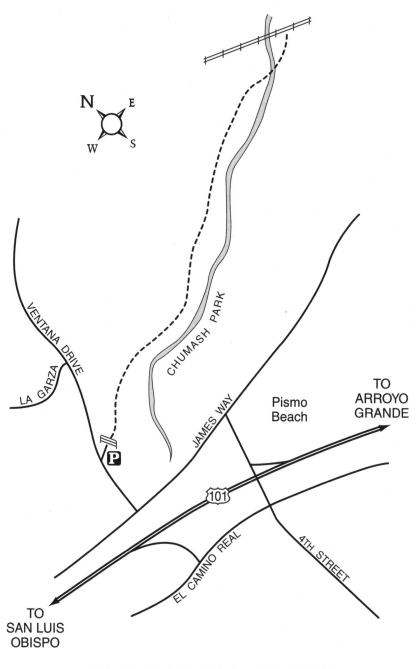

CHUMASH PARK

Hike 59
Monarch Butterfly Grove
and Meadow Creek Trail

Hiking distance: 1.5 miles round trip
Hiking time: 1 hour
Elevation gain: Level
Maps: U.S.G.S. Pismo and Oceano
　　　　Pismo State Beach map

Summary of hike: The Monarch Butterfly Grove is a wintering home for thousands of butterflies in a picturesque grove of mature eucalyptus trees. From the grove, a short portion of the hike follows Meadow Creek, then runs along the west edge of the golf course. Various side trails lead across the dunes. At the trail's end is a viewing platform with coastline views of the Shell Beach cliffs and Port San Luis.

Driving directions: From Highway 101 in Pismo Beach, take the Pismo Beach/Highway 1 South exit. Take Highway 1 through the town of Pismo Beach (Dolliver Street, which becomes Pacific Boulevard) for 1.4 miles to the parking area along the right side of the road. It is located at the south end of North Beach Campground.

Hiking directions: Walk through the fenced entrance, bearing to the right across the grassy area. The trail loops through the eucalyptus grove, a wintering site for the monarch butterfly. At the far end of the grove, cross the wooden footbridge over Meadow Creek. Follow the creek to the left along the south edge of the campground to a trail split. Both trails lead to the dunes. The left fork follows the perimeter of the golf course to the Meadow Creek Trail. The right fork heads straight for the dunes, then bears left to the Meadow Creek Trail at the northwest boundary of the golf course. The Meadow Creek Trail continues south between the golf course and the dunes. Various side trails curve right into the dunes, then parallel the trail. The trails end at a picnic area at the north entrance to the

Dunes Vehicle Recreation Area, where Grand Avenue meets the ocean. A boardwalk leads out to a coastline viewing platform. Return to the parking lot along the Meadow Creek Trail or over and across the dunes.

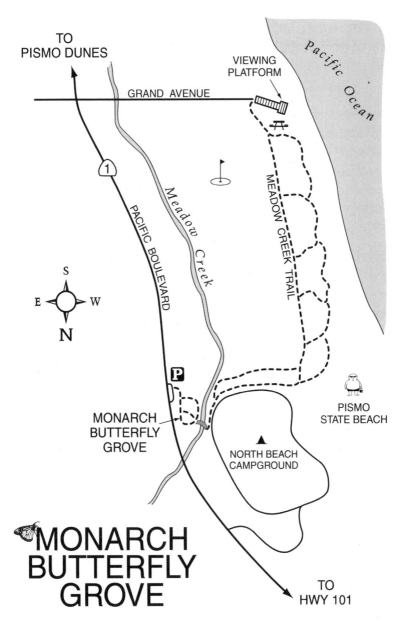

MONARCH BUTTERFLY GROVE

Hike 60
Guiton Trail
Oceano Lagoon

Hiking distance: 1.5 mile loop
Hiking time: 1 hour
Elevation gain: Level
Maps: U.S.G.S. Oceano
      Pismo State Beach map

Summary of hike: The Guiton Trail circles the Oceano Lagoon, a tranquil freshwater lagoon. The trail is named for Harold E. Guiton who donated five acres of lagoon property to the state parks in the mid-1930s. The lagoon is a popular spot for fishing, canoeing and bird watching. The lush riparian habitat creates a secluded pastoral stroll through a forested canopy of Monterey pines, eucalyptus and willows.

Driving directions: From Highway 101 in Pismo Beach, take the Pismo Beach/Highway 1 South exit. Take Highway 1 through the town of Pismo Beach (Dolliver Street, which becomes Pacific Boulevard) for 3 miles to Pier Avenue. Turn right and drive 0.2 miles to the Oceano Campground. Turn right into the campground and park by the nature center on the right.

Hiking directions: Pick up the signed footpath by the lagoon, east of the nature center. Bear left, skirting the eastern edge of the campground along the water's edge. Follow the forested shoreline north, joining a paved path with benches. Curve around the northwest tip of the lagoon where the paved path ends. Loop around the perimeter of the grassy peninsula on the footpath. At the north tip of the lagoon, the trail meets a road at the Parks and Recreation buildings. Bear right, picking up the trail on the east side of the lagoon. Head south through the lush native forest, crossing several footbridges over streams and channels. The trail ends at the bridge on Pier Avenue. Cross the bridge over the lagoon, returning to the nature center.

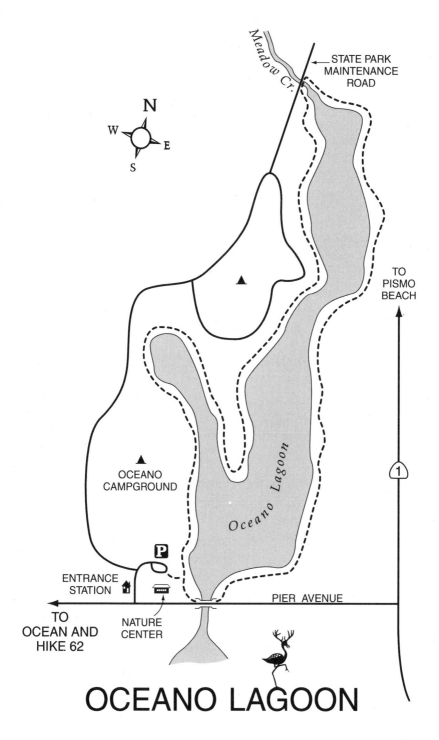

N
W E
S

Meadow Cr.

STATE PARK
MAINTENANCE
ROAD

TO
PISMO
BEACH

① 1

Oceano Lagoon

OCEANO
CAMPGROUND

P

ENTRANCE
STATION

NATURE
CENTER

PIER AVENUE

TO
OCEAN AND
HIKE 62

OCEANO LAGOON

Hike 61
Pismo Dunes

Hiking distance: 2 or more miles round trip
Hiking time: 1 hour
Elevation gain: 100 feet
Maps: U.S.G.S. Oceano
      Pismo State Beach map

Summary of hike: The Pismo Dunes Recreation Area is an all-terrain vehicle playground. The hike begins in this area on the hard-packed oceanfront sand. The shoreline can be busy with cars, trucks and various motorized vehicles. A short distance ahead, the trail enters the undeveloped peaceful solitude of the most extensive coastal dunes in California. The hike meanders through the quiet and fragile natural preserve, crossing scrub-covered, wind-sculpted dunes.

Driving directions: From Highway 101 in Pismo Beach, take the Pismo Beach/Highway 1 South exit. Take Highway 1 through the town of Pismo Beach (Dolliver Street, which becomes Pacific Boulevard) for 3 miles to Pier Avenue. Turn right and drive 0.4 miles to the Pismo Beach State Park parking lot at the beachfront.

Hiking directions: Head south across the hard-packed sand between the ocean and the dunes. Hike 0.3 miles to Arroyo Grande Creek, passing beachfront homes along the way. After crossing the creek, curve to the left, entering the scrub-covered dunes at one of the many access trails. Meander south across the dunes, following the various interconnecting trails. Choose your own turnaround spot. On the return, continue north until reaching Arroyo Grande Creek. Follow the creek west, returning to the beach near the trailhead.

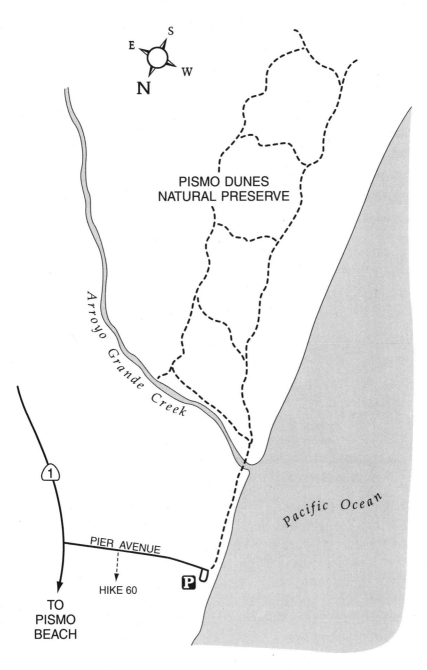

PISMO DUNES
NATURAL PRESERVE

Arroyo Grande Creek

Pacific Ocean

①

PIER AVENUE

HIKE 60

Ⓟ

TO
PISMO
BEACH

PISMO DUNES

Hike 62
Blackberry Springs & Turkey Ridge Loop
Lopez Lake Recreation Area

Hiking distance: 1.8 mile loop
Hiking time: 1 hour
Elevation gain: 420 feet
Maps: U.S.G.S. Tar Spring Ridge
       Lopez Lake Trail Guide

Summary of hike: The Blackberry Springs Trail is an interpretive trail with learning stations that describe the immediate surroundings. The trail winds up a narrow, fern-lined canyon lush with gooseberries, blackberries, poison oak and a fungus-algae draping off the valley oaks. The Turkey Ridge Trail follows a ridge to overlooks with great views of Lopez Lake, the Santa Lucia Mountains, the Sierra Madres and the Caliente Range.

Driving directions: From Highway 101 in Arroyo Grande, take the Grand Avenue exit, and head east through old town Arroyo Grande. At 1 mile, bear right on Huasna Road at the junction with Highway 227. Continue 9.9 miles (staying to the left onto Lopez Drive at a road fork) to the Lopez Lake Recreation Area entrance station. Park at the east end of the parking lot behind the registration office by the Turkey Ridge Trail sign. A parking fee is required.

Hiking directions: Cross the bridge to the north into the Squirrel Campground. Walk up the campground road 50 yards to the signed Blackberry Springs Trail on the left. Head up the steps and wind through the forest, bearing right at a junction. The trail descends into a secluded glen, then follows the shady canyon floor up the lush drainage. Long, wide steps head steeply uphill to a T-junction with the High Ridge Trail at 0.8 miles (Hike 64). Bear right 20 yards to the Turkey Ridge Trail on the left. Go left, heading uphill to an overlook. The trail curves right, traversing the edge of the mountain to several more overlooks. Switchbacks lead back to the parking lot.

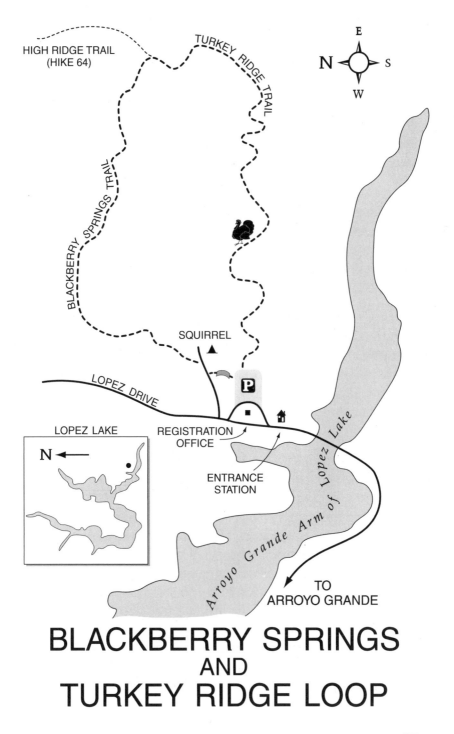

BLACKBERRY SPRINGS
AND
TURKEY RIDGE LOOP

Hike 63
Cougar Trail
Lopez Lake Recreation Area

Hiking distance: 3.4 miles round trip
Hiking time: 1.5 hours
Elevation gain: 150 feet
Maps: U.S.G.S. Tar Spring Ridge
Lopez Lake Trail Guide

Summary of hike: The Cougar Trail is a connector trail between five campgrounds. It skirts the eastern border of the campgrounds parallel to the Wittenberg Arm of Lopez Lake. The trail winds across the pastoral rolling grasslands and oak woodlands.

Driving directions: From Highway 101 in Arroyo Grande, take the Grand Avenue exit, and head east through old town Arroyo Grande. At 1 mile, bear right on Huasna Road at the junction with Highway 227. Continue 9.9 miles (staying to the left onto Lopez Drive at a road fork) to the Lopez Lake Recreation Area entrance station. Park in the lot next to the registration office. A parking fee is required.

Hiking directions: Walk 30 yards north to the signed trailhead by the right side of the park road. Head north across the rolling hills. Skirt around the perimeter of the Eagle Campground. The trail exits into the Cougar Campground. Follow the road to the right, and pick up the signed trail again on the right. Continue winding through the forested rolling hills past the eastern edge of the Quail Campground. Climb the hill and loop around the east and north side of the Mustang Campground and the waterslide. Once over the hill, the trail descends around the Escondido Campground. The path ends at Lopez Drive (the park road) at the Arboleda picnic area. To return, retrace your steps or follow the park road back to the trailhead.

To hike further, head north on the park road to connect with the Wittenberg Trail (Hike 66) and the High Ridge Trail (Hike 64).

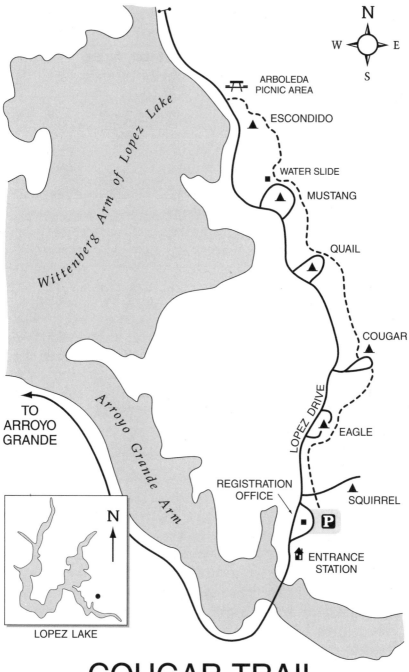

N
W   E
S

ARBOLEDA
PICNIC AREA

ESCONDIDO

WATER SLIDE

MUSTANG

QUAIL

COUGAR

Wittenberg Arm of Lopez Lake

Arroyo Grande Arm

LOPEZ DRIVE

TO
ARROYO
GRANDE

EAGLE

REGISTRATION
OFFICE

SQUIRREL

P

ENTRANCE
STATION

N

LOPEZ LAKE

COUGAR TRAIL

Hike 64
High Ridge Trail
Lopez Lake Recreation Area

Hiking distance: 5 miles round trip
Hiking time: 2.5 hours
Elevation gain: 450 feet
Maps: U.S.G.S. Tar Spring Ridge
Lopez Lake Trail Guide

Summary of hike: The High Ridge Trail follows a firebreak along the east ridge of the recreation area above Lopez Lake. The trail passes a series of steep canyons. There are spectacular views of the lake and surrounding mountains from the ridge. Along the trail are scattered fossils of scallops, sand dollars and oysters in the sedimentary rocks.

Driving directions: From Highway 101 in Arroyo Grande, take the Grand Avenue exit, and head east through old town Arroyo Grande. At 1 mile, bear right on Huasna Road at the junction with Highway 227. Continue 9.9 miles (staying to the left onto Lopez Drive at a road fork) to the Lopez Lake Recreation Area entrance station. Park at the east end of the parking lot behind the registration office by the Turkey Ridge Trail sign. A parking fee is required.

Hiking directions: Take the Turkey Ridge Trail up the hillside on the narrow footpath. Head up through oak groves to a grassy overlook at 0.7 miles by a trail split. Continue straight ahead and down the switchbacks. Head uphill again to a junction with the High Ridge Trail at 1.1 mile. Bear right, passing the Blackberry Springs Trail on the left (Hike 62). Follow the roller-coaster ridge on the wide firebreak. At two miles, pass the Bobcat Trail on the left. At 2.7 miles, stay right at two junctions leading down to the Escondido Campground. Just beyond a massive sandstone outcropping is an unsigned junction in an oak grove. Bear left, curving downhill to the Wittenberg Trail near the lake. Head left along the park road 1.5 miles back to the trailhead.

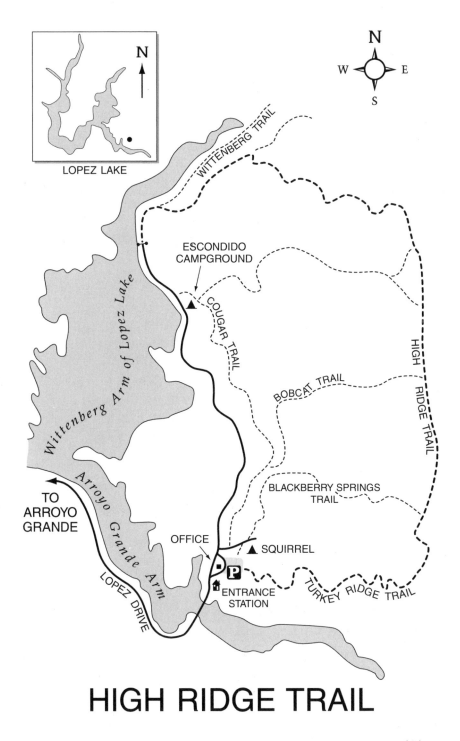

LOPEZ LAKE

N

W E

S

WITTENBERG TRAIL

ESCONDIDO
CAMPGROUND

COUGAR TRAIL

BOBCAT TRAIL

HIGH RIDGE TRAIL

Wittenberg Arm of Lopez Lake

Arroyo Grande Arm

BLACKBERRY SPRINGS
TRAIL

TO
ARROYO
GRANDE

LOPEZ DRIVE

OFFICE

P

SQUIRREL

ENTRANCE
STATION

TURKEY RIDGE TRAIL

HIGH RIDGE TRAIL

Hike 65
Marina and Rocky Point Trails
Lopez Lake Recreation Area

Hiking distance: 1.5 miles round trip
Hiking time: 1 hour
Elevation gain: 120 feet
Maps: U.S.G.S. Tar Spring Ridge
   Lopez Lake Trail Guide

Summary of hike: The Marina Trail climbs over a forested 160-foot hill dividing the park entrance from the marina. The Rocky Peak Trail intersects the Marina Trail, leading to the tip of the peninsula at a flat, slab rock overlook. There are great views of Lopez Lake and the surrounding mountains.

Driving directions: From Highway 101 in Arroyo Grande, take the Grand Avenue exit, and head east through old town Arroyo Grande. At 1 mile, bear right on Huasna Road at the junction with Highway 227. Continue 9.9 miles (staying to the left onto Lopez Drive at a road fork) to the Lopez Lake Recreation Area entrance station. Drive 100 yards to the Valley Oak Picnic Area. Turn left and park. A fee is required.

Hiking directions: Head up the grassy hill past the Marina Trail sign and the feeding stable. Cross the oak woodland up to a ridge with a bench and four-way junction. This junction is the return point to hike all three trails. Begin on the left fork, heading south on the Rocky Point Trail. The trail curves around the forested hillside. Descend through an oak grove to the tip of the peninsula, overlooking the lake on three sides. This is a great spot for bird watching, sunbathing, fishing or daydreaming. At low water, fisherman trails lead down to the shoreline. Return to the four-way junction and take the Marina Trail west. This path ends at another rocky point overlooking Lopez Lake and the mountains to the west. Back at the junction, the Rocky Point Trail heads north through an oak grove to Marina Road. Return to the four-way junction and head east back to trailhead.

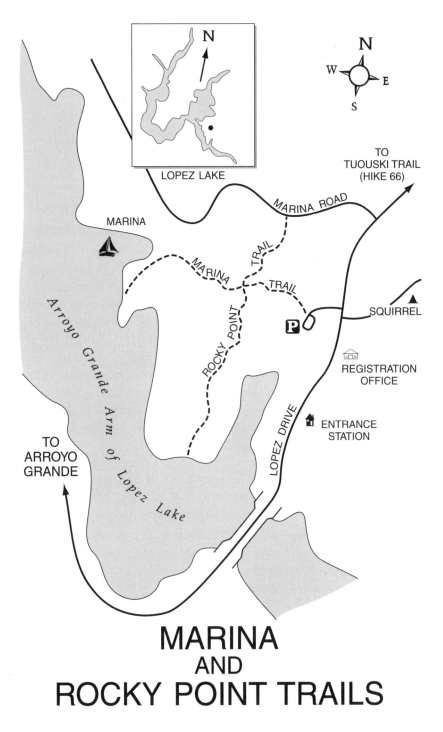

N

LOPEZ LAKE

N
W E
S

TO
TUOUSKI TRAIL
(HIKE 66)

MARINA

MARINA ROAD

MARINA TRAIL

TRAIL

SQUIRREL

ROCKY POINT

P

REGISTRATION
OFFICE

Arroyo Grande Arm of Lopez Lake

LOPEZ DRIVE

ENTRANCE
STATION

TO
ARROYO
GRANDE

MARINA
AND
ROCKY POINT TRAILS

Hike 66
Tuouski and Two Waters Trails to Duna Vista
Lopez Lake Recreation Area

Hiking distance: 7 miles round trip
Hiking time: 3 hours
Elevation gain: 650 feet
Maps: U.S.G.S. Tar Spring Ridge
Lopez Lake Trail Guide

Summary of hike: Duna Vista is a 1,178-foot summit overlook with 360-degree views that include Lopez Lake, the Pacific Ocean, Pismo Dunes and the Santa Lucia Mountains. The hike to Duna Vista begins on the picturesque Wittenberg Trail along the shores of the Wittenberg Arm of Lopez Lake. The Tuouski Trail follows the oak studded hills along the Wittenberg Arm through hollows and over ridges. The Two Waters Trail crosses the peninsula that separates the arms of Lopez Lake. The Duna Vista Trail climbs the ridge to a prominence with benches.

Driving directions: Follow the driving directions for Hike 65 to the Lopez Lake Recreation Area entrance station. Continue 1.3 miles up Lopez Drive and park on the right near the end of the road. A parking fee is required.

Hiking directions: Hike 100 yards north on the paved road to the locked gate. Pass the gate on the level, unpaved road along the lakeshore. Hike past the High Ridge Trail (Hike 64) on the right. At 0.9 miles, bear left along the fenceline past French Camp, following the signs to the Tuouski Trail. Take the signed trail—a footpath winding through the forest on the bluffs. The trail curves along the contours of the hills overlooking Lopez Lake. At 2.3 miles is a signed junction. Take the Two Waters Trail to the right. Switchbacks lead 0.7 miles up to a saddle at another signed junction. Take the Duna Vista Trail to the left up the ridge between the Lopez and Wittenberg Arms. In a half mile, the path reaches Duna Vista on a knoll with three benches. After savoring the views, return a short distance and take the

Tuouski Trail on the right. Descend 1.3 miles, completing the loop back at the Two Waters Trail junction. Stay to the right along the Wittenberg Arm, returning on the same path.

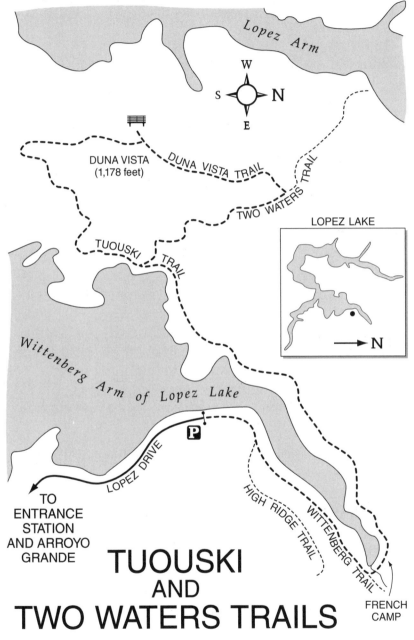

TUOUSKI
AND
TWO WATERS TRAILS

Hike 67
Little Falls Trail

Hiking distance: 1 mile round trip
Hiking time: 30 minutes
Elevation gain: 100 feet
Maps: U.S.G.S. Tar Spring Ridge and Santa Margarita Lake
       Mountain Biking Eastern SLO County

Summary of hike: Little Falls is a beautiful 50-foot waterfall in a lush limestone-walled canyon covered with moss and ferns. At the base of the falls is a circular 2—3 foot deep pool. The Little Falls Trail follows Little Creek through a forest of oak, maple, sycamore and bay trees. The falls is in the Santa Lucia Wilderness north of Lopez Lake.

Driving directions: From Highway 101 in Arroyo Grande, take the Grand Avenue exit, and head east through old town Arroyo Grande. At 1 mile, bear right on Huasna Road at the junction with Highway 227. Continue 9.8 miles (staying to the left onto Lopez Drive at a road fork) to Hi Mountain Road, located just before the Lopez Lake entrance station. Turn right and drive 0.8 miles to a road fork. Bear left on Upper Lopez Canyon Road, and drive 6.4 miles to the end of the paved road. Turn right and take the dirt road 1.5 miles, crossing Lopez Creek 8 times, to the signed trailhead on the right. Park in the pullout on the left.

Hiking directions: Head north past the trail sign on the left side of Little Falls Creek. Cross the creek to the signed Santa Lucia Wilderness boundary. Follow the trail across the flat, grassy meadow through an oak grove. Head into the wooded canyon, crossing Little Falls Creek three more times. At the next crossing, the Little Falls Trail heads up the hillside above the creek. Before crossing the creek, bear left, leaving the main trail. Scramble 50 yards up the rocky canyon, following the creek upstream to Little Falls. The last 20 yards involves wading up the stream to the pool at the base of the falls.

To hike further, cross the creek on the Little Falls Trail, continuing north past numerous rock-sculpted, streamside pools and creek crossings. At 2.6 miles, the Little Falls Trail ends at Hi Mountain Road, where the Rinconada Trail begins (Hike 51). To return, retrace your steps.

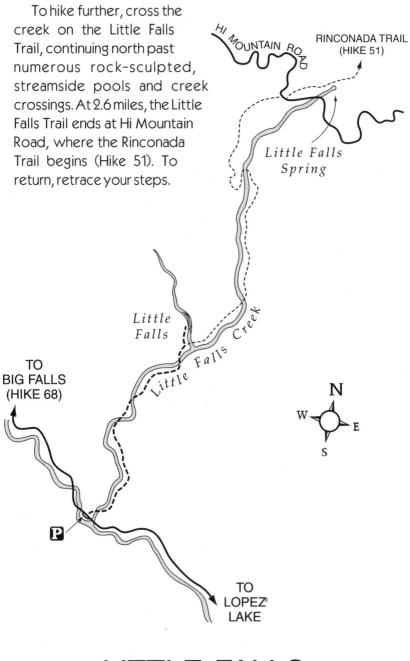

LITTLE FALLS

Hike 68
Big Falls Trail

Hiking distance: 3 miles round trip
Hiking time: 1.5 hours
Elevation gain: 350 feet
Maps: U.S.G.S. Lopez Mountain
  Mountain Biking Eastern SLO County

Summary of hike: Big Falls is an 80-foot cataract in the isolated Santa Lucia Wilderness north of Lopez Lake. The trail follows Big Falls Creek up the wooded canyon, crossing and recrossing the creek. Along the way is an impressive 40-foot double waterfall over limestone rock. At the top and base of this lower falls are beautiful pools.

Driving directions: From Highway 101 in Arroyo Grande, take the Grand Avenue exit, and head east through old town Arroyo Grande. At 1 mile, bear right on Huasna Road at the junction with Highway 227. Continue 9.8 miles (staying to the left onto Lopez Drive at a road fork) to Hi Mountain Road, just before the Lopez Lake entrance station. Turn right and drive 0.8 miles to a road fork. Bear left on Upper Lopez Canyon Road, and drive 6.4 miles to the end of the paved road. Turn right and drive 3.7 miles on the dirt road, crossing Lopez Creek 13 times. Park in the pullout on the right across from two waterfalls.

Hiking directions: Take the trail on the right and rock hop over Lopez Creek. Head north, following Big Falls Creek upstream through the lush, forested canyon. Continue past pools, cascades and several more creek crossings. At 0.5 miles, bear left on an unsigned side trail before crossing the creek. A short distance ahead on this side path is a circular pool at the base of the lower falls. Return to the main trail and cross the creek, heading deeper into Big Falls Canyon. The trail recrosses the creek several more times and traverses the east-facing canyon wall. At 1.3 miles, the trail meets the creek. Stay to the left (west) of the creek past a series of small waterfalls and rock pools. Big Falls can be spotted from a spur trail bearing left. The left fork descends to the base of Big Falls and a large pool. Return along the same trail.

To hike further, the trail continues for another mile, ascending up and out of the canyon to Hi Mountain Road.

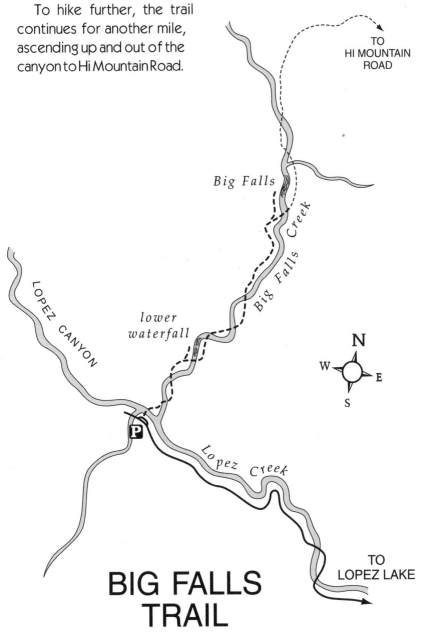

TO
HI MOUNTAIN
ROAD

Big Falls

Big Falls Creek

LOPEZ CANYON

lower waterfall

N
W E
S

P

Lopez Creek

TO
LOPEZ LAKE

BIG FALLS TRAIL

Hike 69
Hi Mountain Trail

Hiking distance: 4 mile loop
Hiking time: 2 hours
Elevation gain: 600 feet
Maps: U.S.G.S. Tar Spring Ridge and Caldwell Mesa
        Mountain Biking Eastern SLO County

Summary of hike: The Hi Mountain Trail is a multiuse trail in the Los Padres National Forest east of Lopez Lake. The trail heads up the canyon in a shaded riparian forest parallel to a stream. While climbing out of the canyon, there are several spectacular vistas. The hike returns on an unpaved road, winding through the pastoral oak-dotted hills of the upper Arroyo Grande valley.

Driving directions: From Highway 101 in Arroyo Grande, take the Grand Avenue exit, and head east through old town Arroyo Grande. At 1 mile, bear right on Huasna Road at the junction with Highway 227. Continue 9.8 miles (staying to the left onto Lopez Drive at a road fork) to Hi Mountain Road, located just before the Lopez Lake entrance station. Turn right and drive 5.5 miles (bearing right at the Upper Lopez Canyon Road fork) to the signed trailhead parking area on the left.

Hiking directions: Hike past the trailhead gate, heading north on the wide grassy path. Enter a shaded oak forest on the right side of a trickling stream. At 0.3 miles, cross over the seasonal stream and again at a half mile, continuing gently uphill through the lush canyon. A short distance ahead, switchbacks lead away from the drainage and up the east wall of the canyon to a grassy flat overlooking the canyon and surrounding mountains. Cross the open hillside, then climb steeply to a saddle. Bear left to a knoll with a 360-degree view. Descend to the right towards Hi Mountain Road. Cross the meadow to the road. Bear right on the narrow road through rolling hills and oak groves for 1.9 miles back to the trailhead.

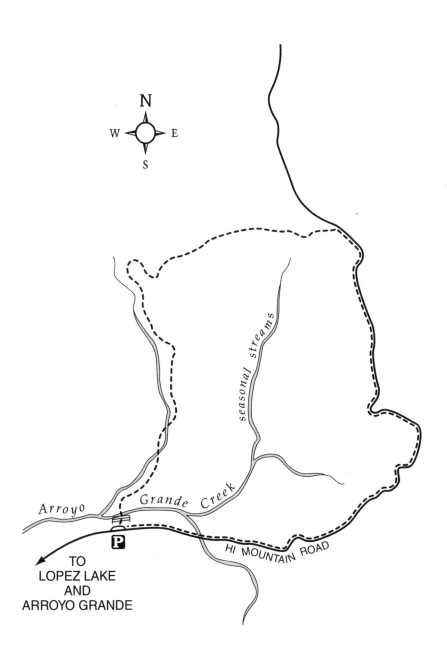

N
W E
S

seasonal streams

Arroyo Grande Creek

HI MOUNTAIN ROAD

P

TO
LOPEZ LAKE
AND
ARROYO GRANDE

HI MOUNTAIN TRAIL

Hike 70
Trout Creek Trail

Hiking distance: 6 miles round trip
Hiking time: 3 hours
Elevation gain: 250 feet
Maps: U.S.G.S. Santa Margarita Lake, Pozo Summit, and
Caldwell Mesa
Mountain Biking Eastern SLO County

Summary of hike: The Trout Creek Trail is a quiet back-country trail in the Los Padres National Forest. The meandering, near-level hike winds through meadows and oak forests. The trail parallels and crosses Trout Creek nine times up the canyon. The trail is primarily used as an equestrian route.

Driving directions: From Highway 101 in Arroyo Grande, take the Grand Avenue exit, and head east through old town Arroyo Grande. At 1 mile, bear right on Huasna Road at the junction with Highway 227. Continue 9.8 miles (staying to the left onto Lopez Drive at a road fork) to Hi Mountain Road, located just before the Lopez Lake entrance station. Turn right and drive 6.2 miles (bearing right at the Upper Lopez Canyon Road fork) to the end of the paved road. Continue 5.4 miles on the narrow, winding unpaved road to the Trout Creek pullout on the right. If you reach the large wooden Los Padres National Forest sign, return 0.1 mile to the trailhead.

Hiking directions: Head east on the signed trail parallel to Trout Creek. The trail alternates from an oak forest canopy to grassy meadows throughout the hike with frequent creek crossings. After the ninth crossing, follow a narrow cliffside trail on the left side of Trout Creek to an unsigned junction with the trail to Buckeye Camp on the left. Stay on the main trail along the creek. The trail ends in less than a half mile at a signed private property boundary. This is the turnaround spot. Return along the same route.

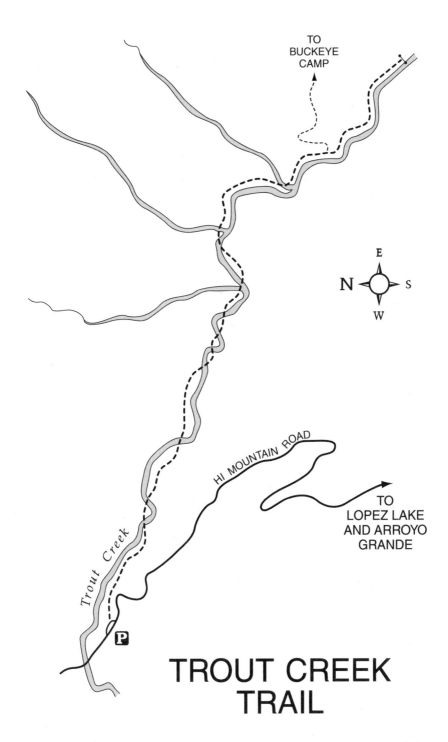

TO
BUCKEYE
CAMP

E
N—◇—S
W

HI MOUNTAIN ROAD

TO
LOPEZ LAKE
AND ARROYO
GRANDE

Trout Creek

P

TROUT CREEK
TRAIL

Hike 71
Oso Flaco Lake Trail

Hiking distance: 2.2 miles round trip
Hiking time: 1 hour
Elevation gain: Level
Maps: U.S.G.S. Oceano
       Oso Flaco Lake Natural Area map

Summary of hike: Oso Flaco Lake is located at the south end of the Pismo Dunes Natural Preserve. The trail crosses a footbridge over the 75-acre lake and wetlands preserve. The freshwater lake is surrounded by cattails, sedges, wax myrtle and willows. It is a great place for watching birds and wildlife. A wooden boardwalk leads through the Nipomo Dunes and wetland area, minimizing damage to the fragile plant life. The boardwalk ends at the ocean.

Driving directions: From Highway 101 in Nipomo, take the Tefft Street exit, and head 0.8 miles west to Orchard Road. Turn left and drive 0.7 miles to Division Street. Turn right and continue 3.2 miles to Oso Flaco Lake Road. Bear right and go 5.3 miles to the Oso Flaco Lake parking lot at the end of the road. A parking fee is required.

Hiking directions: Head west on the paved road past the trailhead gate and through the shady cottonwood forest to the shores of Oso Flaco Lake. Bear left on the long footbridge spanning the lake. From the west end of the lake, continue on a wooden boardwalk that ambles across the fragile coastal dunes. Most of the trail follows the boardwalk except for a short, well-marked sandy stretch. The boardwalk ends at the ocean on a long and wide stretch of sandy beach at 1.1 mile. To the south is the Mobil Coastal Preserve and Coreopsis Hill, a large dune. To the north is the Pismo Dunes (Hike 61) and the Santa Maria River. Explore at your own pace up and down the coastline. Return on the boardwalk.

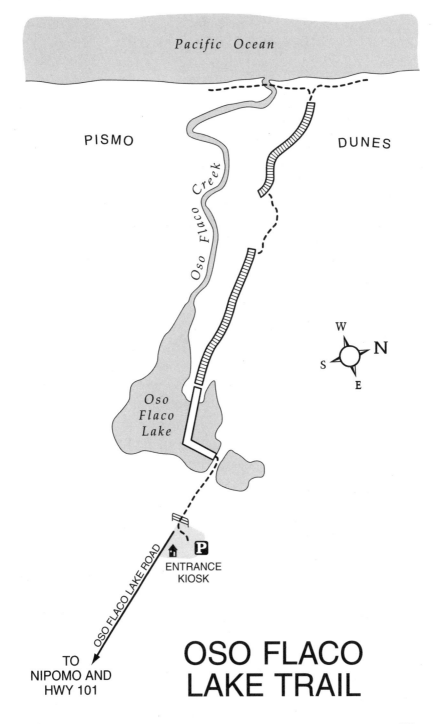

OSO FLACO LAKE TRAIL

Hike 72
Nipomo Regional Park

Hiking distance: 2 miles round trip
Hiking time: 1 hour
Elevation gain: 50 feet
Maps: U.S.G.S. Nipomo
       Nipomo Regional Park map
       The Thomas Guide—San Luis Obispo County

Summary of hike: Nipomo Regional Park encompasses more than 140 acres with 80 backcountry acres. The southeast end of the park is developed with multiple baseball fields and a picnic area. At the northeast end is a 12-acre native garden area with a short nature trail through oak savanna and chaparral. The balance of the park is undeveloped with only hiking and equestrian trails.

Driving directions: From Highway 101 in Nipomo, take the Tefft Street exit, and head 0.5 miles west to Pomeroy Road. Turn right and drive 0.2 miles to the Nipomo Regional Park parking lot on the left. Turn left and park in the second lot on the left.

Hiking directions: Cross the park road and pick up the unsigned trail heading northwest. Cross the grassy flat under the ponderosa pines, and follow the sandy trail up the gentle slope. A short distance ahead is a trail split. None of the trail forks are signed. The right fork drops over the hillside and winds to the north end of the park by the native gardens. The left fork meanders through the chaparral and oak trees to additional trail splits. All of the trails interconnect, weaving through the natural area. Choose your own route. It is easy to find your way back.